T0351295

'A Very Fine Gift'

THE FRENCH LIST

'A Very Fine Gift'
and Other Writings
on **Theory**

Roland Barthes

Essays and Interviews,
Volume **1**

TRANSLATION AND

EDITORIAL COMMENTS

BY CHRIS TURNER

LONDON NEW YORK CALCUTTA

www.bibliofrance.in

The work is published with the support of the Publication Assistance
Programmes of the Institut français

Seagull Books, 2015

ISBN 978 0 8574 2 226 2

British Library Cataloguing-in-Publication Data
A catalogue record for this book is available from the British Library.

Book designed and typeset by Bishan Samaddar, Seagull Books, Calcutta, Ind
Printed and bound by Maple Press, York, Pennsylvania, USA

Contents

Should Grammar
Be Killed Off?

This article was first published in the Paris-based newspaper *Combat*, being Roland Barthes's second contribution to that publication. *Combat*, which had its origins in the French Resistance movement of the Second World War, represented a popular non-Communist Left and its team of journalists and irregular contributors included such figures as Pascal Pia, Albert Camus, Roger Grenier and Alexandre Astruc (now better known as a film director and critic). It also opened its columns to some other leading writers of the day, including André Gide, André Malraux and Jean-Paul Sartre. At the time of Barthes's first publication in *Combat*, Camus had just resigned (on 3 June 1947) from a second spell as editor. Barthes's own connection with the *Combat* group came through the Trotskyist Georges Fournié. Fournié introduced him to Maurice Nadeau, the Trotskyite critic and early historian of Surrealism, who contributed articles to the newspaper's cultural page.

Unlike the other articles published in *Combat* at this time, this one was not reproduced in *Writing Degree Zero* (1953). It is, rather, a one-off reply to criticisms from

Oeuvres complètes, Volume 1, pp. 96–8

readers of Barthes's preceding article 'Le degré zero de l'écriture' which was published on 1 August 1947. I have restored the original title given to the article in *Combat*, by which it is generally known in the English-speaking world.

The novel *The Reprieve*, mentioned in the article, was the second instalment in Sartre's *Roads to Freedom* trilogy. It was published by Gallimard in 1945.

Not so long ago, literature was still regarded as a craft activity. The writer, who was seen as a kind of home-worker (Victor Hugo's belvedere, Gustave Flaubert's room, Paul Valéry's study in the early morning), had at his disposal a special instrument, French grammar, with which he was supposed to shape his creation as one might model physical material. Grammar represented a salutary technical element in an order of production that was just beginning to be viewed as potentially arbitrary. To write well was both to ensure a certain result and to commit to a certain form of work. Most of the literature that runs from Théophile Gautier to André Gide has a literary labour as its underlying goal.

Moreover, this formal work on the part of the writer matched up with a more general historical purpose. To believe in a single grammar and to write a *pure* French was to persist in the famous myth of French clarity, the destiny of which is so closely bound up with the political history of France. It is quite revealing to date the birth of this myth. In 1647, according to Claude Favre de Vaugelas, to be clear was to speak as they spoke at court. Clarity was correct usage or, in other words, the usage of the social group directly associated with political rule. After 1660, however, monarchical authority was sufficiently strong for the transition to be made from cynicism to hypocrisy, an all-too-familiar transformation in history. Clarity, which ten years earlier was accepted as merely being the usage of the most powerful, now set itself up as something universal. The Port-Royal grammar no longer justified its rules on grounds of usage but of the logical attunement between those rules and the demands of the mind.

All the commentators on this period, even the modern ones, set great store by the reforms of the seventeenth century, which aimed to produce a language so clear that it could be understood by everyone. But that 'everyone' has only ever been a tiny portion of the nation. And, moreover, it was in the name of a demand for universality that the words and syntax intelligible to the people—those of work and action—were excluded from the language. There has doubtless been a certain universality of writing style that has stretched across elites dispersed throughout Europe, all enjoying the same privileged mode of life, but the much-vaunted communicability of the French language has only ever been a horizontal phenomenon. It has not been vertical. It has never penetrated into the deeper reaches of the social mass.

Classical French, the only instrument currently available to literature—except where it resorts to even more esoteric techniques—is, first and foremost, the language of a powerful group, or a leisured one, or one engaged in a special kind of work we might describe as managerial. An infinite range of actions are necessarily excluded from that language, as is action itself, which continues to exist there only as a deep, visceral mode of feeling. Hence, among other things, the primacy of tenses, the disappearance of modes and, in general, all the technical reforms that can help to eliminate from the language of *society's leaders*, as we might say now, that very special subjectivity of the man of the people, a subjectivity that is always determined through an action, not through thinking.

Now, since the—it must be said—entirely political formulation of our classical language, no serious rhetorical revolution, including the Romantic and Symbolist revolutions, has swept away the sham claim of a language to be universal, when in fact it is merely privileged. Revolutions in language, all of them exclusively literary, are greatly over-rated; they come down in the end to waves of reticence towards, or infatuation with, certain secondary writing techniques. They are never anything more than, in Hugo's guileless phrase, storms in an inkwell. Saint-Just spoke the language of [François] Fénelon; Gide, [François] Mauriac and

[Georges] Duhamel followed the grammar of Port-Royal, and [Albert] Camus himself writes a novel more or less the way Flaubert and Stendhal did. The fact that classical grammar has, within its limited social ambit, achieved a certain degree of perfection must not be allowed to hide the enormous sacrifices that the exclusive use of such an instrument costs us with regard to the expression of a human totality—and perhaps even the formation of new ideas.

The problem for today's writers is, then, to cut language off from its historical origins, which means, in fact, its political origins. It seems, even now, that substantial areas of normative grammar are at times being abandoned, together with some time-honoured mannerisms (except where it is still necessary to appeal to a—actually quite embarrassing—traditional audience). Above all, the very idea of a normative writing style is being abandoned. Our most perceptive writers understand that there are, in fact, as many grammars as social groups and act accordingly. For today's writer, to write well increasingly means to have perfect knowledge of the multiplicity of these grammars which vary subtly and almost imperceptibly in their social reach. This is the only possible objective path. But for all that *speech* plays an increasingly important role in literary creation, it cannot entirely eliminate the necessarily conventional part of literary language that is narration.

This is the last bastion of classical grammar. It is the most critical point in the style impasse, the impasse around which our writers are becoming most sensitive, combative and inventive. Effort upon effort is being made to wrest narration from its deadly literary strait-jacket. As soon as they are able, writers substitute monologue for narration or create secondary subjectivities within the narrative, since what is presented as dream or memory looks ultimately to be more objectively written than what is presented as narrative. As in *The Reprieve*, they adopt a simultaneous narration so as to break the hold of a monolingual narrative. The writer's field of action is extended into the theatre or cinema. Stumbling—and rightly so—over this problem of writing, literature is tending to break up, to break out or, at any rate, to shift its ground. The writer is beginning to cheat with the language handed down to him by his condition and traditions. When [Jean-Paul] Sartre, for example, turns his hand to screenplays, he is probably not doing so in order to dabble in multiple genres, after the dilettantish fashion of a [Jean] Cocteau. We have here, rather, the beginnings of a shift of literature away from the verbal instrument that was its pride and joy for three centuries but is now a growing source of unease as the existence of distinct social groups becomes increasingly apparent to the contemporary writer.

Combat (26 September 1947)

A Brief Sociology of the Contemporary French Novel

This article was published in February 1955 in *Documents*, a publication subtitled *A Monthly Review of Franco-German Questions*, which is not to be confused with the literary review of the same name that ran from 1929 to 1931 (and was very much associated with Georges Bataille). Interest in the *sociology* of literature—and, particularly, in mass-market literature—marks Barthes out as something of a pioneer. For comparison, Lucien Goldmann had published little on the subject at this point, his major work *Le Dieu caché* (The Hidden God) not appearing in French until later in 1955; Richard Hoggart's *The Uses of Literacy* did not find its way into print until 1957; while Robert Escarpit's *Sociologie de la Littérature* was published in 1958.

Oeuvres complètes, Volume 1, pp. 555–62

Despite some local efforts to escape the iron law of the system (I have in mind the paternalistic or cooperative spirit of certain publishing houses), it is perfectly clear that our novels are produced and consumed by a society that is capitalist in its nature. I shall confine myself, in this connection, to reminding the reader of the basic characteristics of our literary economy:

1. The tyranny of the corporate distributors.

2. The subordination of the body of producers (the novelists) to the body of distributors. Royalties are, most often, waged employment in disguise.

3. The subordination of the literary 'commodity' to the advertising system, whether overt or 'mythified' in the form of literary prizes.

4. The plurality and isolation of the audiences for the novel. Literary 'products' are *tailored* to their consumers; so there is a top-of-the-range literature and a mass literature, and the [sentimental] novels of Marie-Anne Desmarest and the ['serious'] novels of Jean-Claude Brisville are consumed as differently as a bar of Palmolive soap and one produced by the elite perfume house of Guerlain.

We are aware then, on this basis, that the sociology we have to describe cannot but be *differential*. Our task is to establish a relationship between the content of certain novels, which for convenience we will sum up in an archetype, and the particular social groups that consume them. We shall enquire lastly what becomes of the writer when he has to contend with this plurality and this audience segmentation.

However, before setting about a positive classification of audiences for the novel, we must state very clearly that, despite the simplicity of the basic schema, the reality is clearly very complex. On top of the social compartmentalization of novel audiences, there are specific grids of lesser importance which, when applied in combination, make up the particular physiognomy of the audience for each novel. What are these grids?

1. The basic grid is clearly a social one. Its essential elements are:

   (a) Social class. We must beware here of some genuine ambiguities: for example, some fractions of the proletariat may take on the cultural norms of the petty bourgeoisie. Conversely, the upper bourgeoisie may produce a protest group, the intellectuals. The notion of social class, though fundamentally valid, must in certain cases be more closely specified by 'cultural' corrections of this kind.

   (b) Education, level and type of culture.

(c) Place of residence. Transport problems between home and workplace may have an impact on reading—a lot of reading is done in the metro and on suburban trains. There is certainly also much more reading done in the provinces than in Paris. 'Quantity' here may lead to readers extending the scope of their reading or gradually modify the cultural identity of the user.

(d) Working conditions. Tiredness, emotional commitment to work, the conditions for integration into the occupational milieu and the competition from other 'distractions' may, within a single social class, cause variations in the extent to which work impinges on leisure. The phenomenon of reading changes according to occupational context.

2. An anthropological grid: readerships of women, readerships of young people.

3. A psycho-social grid, in which the main elements might be:

(a) Political or religious activism. It is, for example, certain that in the bourgeoisie in general there is a particular readership characterized by the reading of works by [Jacques] Chardonne, [André] Fraigneau, [Roger] Nimier, [Antoine] Blondin and [Jacques] Laurent that are united around a particular ideology which is a kind of declared, activist 'right-wing' position.

(b) 'Bits and pieces'. Naturism, exoticism, sport, detective novels. There are definitely specialist readerships based around novelists defined by a particular 'specialism': novels of the sea ([Édouard] Peisson), novels set in Indochina ([Jean] Hougron).

4. A seasonal grid. A readership for prize-winning novels, fashions arising out of certain topical events, readerships drawn to a particular book as a result of a successful cinema adaptation (for example, George Arnaud's *The Wages of Fear* [1950]).

The analysis of each of these grids would require careful investigation and, to my knowledge, such studies have not yet been carried out in France. Here I shall simply give a very rough picture of the groups that fall within the scope of the first grid, though this one—the social grid—is, in my view, the most important. Naturally, this is only a working hypothesis, not a scientific presentation of the question.

*

I shall describe three readership groups, providing for each a novelistic archetype, the order of magnitude of print runs, the distribution network, the social class, the basic myths and the criticism normally directed towards the group's novelistic production.

I shall provide two archetypes in this instance: (a) the novels of Delly or novels for girls; (b) Marie-Anne Desmarest's novel *Torrents* (1938).

These novels have substantial print runs, in the region of several hundred thousand copies per author and even, in the case of *Torrents*, for example, per book.

The typical publishing houses involved are Plon or Denoël.

The readership for these novels is very precisely that of women's magazines. Both the magazines and the novels meet the same mythic need which we might define using [Albert] Thibaudet's phrase: 'The novel is where love is.' What we have here, in fact, is a genuinely institutionalized feminine literature which has its own laws of operation, set of themes and morality. Socially, the majority of this particular audience comes from the impecunious petty bourgeoisie. Female office workers, secretaries, typists, saleswomen and lower-ranking female civil servants form the bulk of the group, representing all in all the female equivalent of the 'white-collar proletariat'. However, one of the forms of complexity I mentioned above lies in the fact that the readership also contains, alongside this proletarianized element, a fraction of leisured women from the rich bourgeoisie (nouveaux riches, wives of big businessmen).

The essential myth of this literature is obviously Love. To take our two archetypes: in Delly's novels that love is always chaste, the only manifestation of evil in those books being rivalry, a fateful force wholly unrelated to sin. In the *Torrents*-type novel, by contrast, a certain eroticism is present. The evil here is of the order of the peccadillo, taking the form not of rivalry but of infidelity. Bad, sensuous characters appear in these novels, such as the wicked woman, the novelistic counterpart of the fortune teller's Queen of Spades. This same difference is also reflected in the denouements of the two types. In the Delly-type novel, the happy ending is merely a restoration of an innocent human nature that was momentarily overwhelmed by a series of unfortunate circumstances. In the *Torrents*-type novel, the happy ending doesn't restore an unblemished innocence—the 'slate is wiped clean' with regard to a transgression on the heroine's part, leaving her more 'mature' or, in other words, bearing the marks of an 'experience of life'.

This literature doesn't fall within the purview of literary criticism. However, new books are 'launched' through reviews in women's magazines such as *Les Bonnes Soirées* which has a substantial circulation.

2. BOURGEOIS NOVELS

As archetypes of this novels-readership complex, I shall take the works of Henri Troyat, Paul Vialar or, more recently, Michel de Saint-Pierre (*Les Aristocrates* [1954]).

Print runs for these writers are approximately one tenth of what they are for the preceding category, being in the region of tens of thousands of copies. For a long time, a good example of the kind of publisher for these sorts of novels was Grasset. Today, the role seems to have been taken over by Julliard. The readership is more or less the public that is sensitive to the literary 'prizes' and is indeed contributing decisively to the institutionalization of the prize novel. These are readers who buy seven or eight novels a year, including the winners of the three main literary prizes. There is little need for fine social distinctions here. It is a readership formed by what we might call the uncultivated solid middle classes [*bonne bourgeoisie*].

It follows that the standard myths of this literature are the myths of the bourgeoisie itself: the social taboos of 'good' society, family issues, money matters, adultery and ambition. This is essentially a mirroring literature, not one that goes beyond or outside its own milieu. In novels written for the bourgeoisie, that class watches and consumes itself. However, far from involving self-criticism, that watching represents a fixation, seeking as it does to endow the bourgeois microcosm with the triumphant forms of universalism.

Press reviews play an essential role in launching books of this kind, but this is a criticism designed to send the book on its way, not one concerned with its structure; it is a 'moral', not a creative criticism. It is a criticism that strictly represents its class and never attempts to question that class' values. The book is assessed in terms of dated concepts from classical times, concepts entirely consonant with the traditional idea of a universal human essence. 'Style', 'plot', the truth-to-life of 'characters', 'imaginative' powers—these are the elements of this criticism, represented by the reviewers of the *Figaro littéraire* and the *Nouvelles littéraires*, and also the provincial press whose important role should certainly not be forgotten.

3. We come finally to *Literature* properly so called. I shall distinguish between two groups here:

(a) The first group has print runs of up to a few thousand copies. The archetype might be the novels of [André] Dhôtel or the good women's novels, such as those by Dominique Rollin. These novels are read by the poor fraction of the bourgeoisie that is para-intellectual in orientation and made up mainly of state employees such as secondary-school teachers. These are generally works that have the freedom, authenticity and *quality* of literature but differ from the next group I shall describe (and I refuse to present this as a measure of their value) in that they do not challenge the traditional conventions of the novel. They might be said to be works of literary renewal rather than exploration.

(b) The second group could be defined by a recent novel like Michel Henry's *Le Jeune Officier* [1954].

Works in this group must have print runs around 2,000 copies. These are works which seek to move completely beyond literature and aim, in their various ways, to destroy the Aristotelian category of the novel. Traditional notions such as character, plot, psychology and fine style are, as it were, dissolved and replaced by an experimentation of an existential order that attempts to grasp man in the very moment of *making* literature. First and foremost here, the novel is a questioning of the novel. These are works of exploration of the novel form. In Walter Jens' classification they are something like the novels of the *ist*, while Walter Höllerer would speak of *notwendige Romane*.

It is clearly significant that the readership of these novels is made up, above all, of the novelist's 'peers', of a group of writers or intellectuals whom one could describe in some sense as the virtual creators of the work.

These works often suffer at the hands of conventional book reviewers who are accustomed to giving their backing to more 'open' novels, but it may happen that they meet with a structural criticism (in some literary magazine or other) that identifies their importance within the avant-garde.

I have refrained from including in any of these sociological classes a very special novel-readership complex that occupies a place apart in the life of the French nation. I am referring to Communist novels. These are an absolutely autarkic phenomenon of production, distribution and consumption. Communist novels (those by [Pierre] Daix, [Pierre] Courtade, [Pierre] Gamara or André Stil, for example) are written by Communists, published by Communist publishers, read by Communist readers and talked about only by the Communist press. We have to exempt from this the novels of Roger Vailland and Louis Aragon, which find a hearing among bourgeois readers and critics. But these are novelists of bourgeois origin whose subjects are Communist yet whose *art* is not. The quality of their form and their origins enable the bourgeoisie to recognize them and hence to find them reassuring. And, indeed, we shouldn't rule out the possibility that the bourgeois tolerate them because they know that they can compromise them the more easily by doing so.

*

In this way today's French society presents us with highly personalized readerships for novels, but readerships that are also very compartmentalized and isolated and seldom exchange roles. They are determined essentially by the social condition of their members, even when additional 'grids' seem to complicate the question.

This means that works of the mind move within very narrow confines. Only in exceptional cases does a novel travel across the various social strata. It doesn't give anyone an unfamiliar experience; it doesn't *shock* and, more seriously still, *it isn't itself transformed.*

When all is said and done, the novel only ever meets up with *its own* readership, that is to say, with the audience that is in its image, that has a narrow relationship of identity with it. This is a serious feature of the situation, insofar as we may take the view that it is precisely the function of literature to lay before human beings the *lived* image of others. The ideal work is always a work which *astonishes*, and it has to be said that the compartmentalization of readerships can logically only produce works that *reassure.*

This novelistic sociology, which we have just seen to be a sociology of solitude, identity and fixity, should enable us to arrive at a better understanding of a literary phenomenon of great importance in France, the phenomenon of prizes. The literary prize is, as a general rule, a much criticized institution, though it cannot be said to have suffered any great damage as a result. As I see it, the role of prizes is in fact much more ambiguous. In the current state of affairs, given the regrettable separation of social classes, the literary prizes are the only thing capable of upsetting the immutable character of the various readerships, of effecting migrations of any real size from one audience to another, of introducing movement into this enormous, congealed mass of novel readers. Clearly, such a migration is useless, if not indeed harmful, if the book winning the award is bad or meretricious. The potential benefit might then simply turn into a further experience of alienation. Everyone knows that prizes are handed out by a God of Chance which is just another form of servitude. The audience migrations they produce are, therefore, contingent. They are a long way from representing an effort on the part of society to support a literature that is genuinely universalistic in its functioning or expression. So the only massive shifts across different readership categories that we see in France (and the award of a prize may, for example, increase a print run from 2,000 to 100,000 copies) occur blindly.

Against this terribly differential sociology, we are forced, sadly, also to range the loneliness of the creative writer. The pressure of social and economic realities means that he too finds himself in a tremendously closed-off condition. Despite his wishes, he is confined within both a genre that might be termed the Aristotelian novel (what if there are writers who want to write something other than a novel, to create an as-yet-unknown form?) and an audience walled up behind a human otherness that he cannot penetrate; he is shut off, as if within some stifling shell, in a fearful identity with *his own* readership.

Now, sociability is the ontological foundation of the literary act, even when the song it is singing is one of solitude—indeed, particularly when that is the case. Being unable to write for *the others*, the novelist has to pretend he is writing for *someone else*. The alienation of our society is tragically expressed in this last contradiction—at the very point when the world is magnificently disclosing the reality of history, the novelist is still obliged to take refuge in an 'essentialist' image of his reader.

Documents: *Revue mensuelle des questions franco-allemandes*
(February 1955)

An Innovation in Criticism

This book review of Jean-Pierre Richard's *Littérature et sensation* was published in the literary/philosophical journal *Esprit*. Foun-ded by Emmanuel Mounier in the spirit of 1930s Personalism, *Esprit* continued to appear under the Vichy regime until its critical stance caused it to be closed down in August 1941. At the Liberation, it reopened with a more leftward slant and, by the time of this article, its editorship had passed to the Swiss critic Albert Béguin, a close associate of Mounier and one who was, like him, committed to 'free, Christian thought'.

Oeuvres complètes, Volume 1, pp. 622–5

On its publication in 1954, Jean-Pierre Richard's *Littérature et sensation* was des-cribed by Professor Henri Peyre as the most profound work of criticism to appear in France since the war. Richard is often aligned with the Geneva group of critics that includes Georges Poulet, Jean Starobinksi and Albert Béguin and the emphasis of his book is on the intimate experience of the physical world of the various authors under consideration. The interest of Barthes's article perhaps lies in its attempt to suggest that this 'phenom-enological' approach can be subsumed under a fuller—indeed 'total'—historical criticism.

Richard formed part of a web of friendships. Barthes was originally introduced to him in London by Charles Singevin, whom he had known from his time teaching in Alexandria. Richard himself was later to introduce Barthes to Gérard Genette, who became a colleague (at the École pratique) and an ally.

Littérature et Sensation by Jean-Pierre Richard is a felicitous book. That is to say, it is a brilliant, sound, warm-hearted and useful one. It is the usefulness of the book I would like to examine here, because French critics really need to acquire a sense of the complementarity of their efforts and to gauge precisely what use they can make of one another's work.

The critical method employed by Richard is in no sense historical and yet I believe it to be profoundly necessary. Let me explain why. Up to the present, literary criticism has looked only to writers' 'ideas' for evidence of historical determination. To be a historian was necessarily to reduce literature to a series of professions of faith, of aesthetic systems or literary schools, with any element that appeared irreducible being ascribed to 'genius'. This was useful but incomplete. Literature is something more than a pure discourse of ideas. It is defined, in precise terms, by a kind of opacity and, not to mince words, distortion. Literature is, if I may put it this way, distorted philosophy.

Distorted by what? That is the whole question today. For a long time we thought it was distorted by 'style'. We said: there is 'content', which belongs to the field of ideas and of history on the large or small scale, and then there is 'form' which belongs properly to writers and attests to their creative freedom. Richard gives a different definition of the 'specific weight' of literature; going beyond the awkward distinction between thought and style, his criticism regards literary works as the proliferation of a corporeal imagination, as the product of a dialectic between objects—their dimensions and substance—and the writer's body. We are dealing, then, with a genetic criticism, not in terms of chronology but, more profoundly, of the writer's perpetual awakening to literature.

This criticism has, of course, been compared to the 'psychology of matter' sketched out by Sartre and [Gaston] Bachelard (with quite different implications, as Jean Catesson pointed out in a recent article in *Critique*). There is between these authors an undeniable shared sense of critical material—all these analyses assume that same 'unconscious intentionality' in the creative writer that has, in its discovery and use, become a fact of our age. The key factor in Richard's method—and where his innovativeness—lies in taking the writer as someone who genuinely institutes literature and in exploring the substantive psychology of an author in its specificity, its inimitable structure.

The first volume of *Littérature et sensation* (the second, devoted to a number of nineteenth-century poets, will be published shortly[1]) comprises four studies—on Stendhal, Flaubert, [Eugène] Fromentin and the brothers Goncourt. It seems to me that Richard's analyses bring out with great authority the *peculiar characteristics* of each of these authors. In Stendhal's case, this is the way he divides and circumscribes matter, in Flaubert's his passive voraciousness, in Fromentin's the freezing of the landscape and in the Goncourts' the sensuousness and incompleteness of surfaces. Working outward from these central propositions, Richard develops a whole network of explanations and analyses that exhaustively cover the literary (not the conceptual) surface of the writer's works and the range of—infinitely complex—creative acts by which the writer *institutes* literature.

When I said that Richard's book is warm-hearted, I was alluding precisely to the *expansive* character of his criticism. The range of the analyses, the way they gradually reach into all areas of the literary work without ever being destructive of it—that is, the command of a style of commentary directed more at

1 The reader will remember Richard's article 'Rimbaud' that was published by *Esprit* (December 1954–January 1955).

ROLAND BARTHES

revealing what is there than at seeing through it, a criticism we might term tactile—implies the warmth of a supportive, affectionate attitude. *Littérature et sensation* is a book which contributes to a happiness of literature.

Now this is the supreme critical task: to show how the writer uses literature to *look at* history—that is to say, both to manifest it and objectivize it—attempting in a single movement both to give an account of his society and to set himself against it with a kind of marvellous, harrowing corporeal opacity, is *also* part of historical criticism. The historian is no longer simply the person who manages to establish correct lines of causation, he is the one who can see complexities, a whole functional front of facts, of various levels of pressure. Richard's criticism assumes that literature is a complex entity, which is the greatest contribution that can be made today to the history of literature. And since the complexity he reveals is not magical but concrete in nature, we may say that his criticism, empty of history as it is, nonetheless assumes the presence of history in all its irresistible force.

Richard's contribution is, precisely, to turn literary studies from the purely historicizing path (as we know, that leads only to an impasse, since it cannot account for literature without destroying it) and towards a total critical path. This is, no doubt, merely preparatory—Richard's criticism, consisting as it does in a number of monographs, is incomplete. Like all related endeavours, it is quite clearly only a pre-criticism, in keeping indeed with the pre-scientific spirit defined by Bachelard. But the complement it calls for, creates a space for and vindicates, is precisely a deep historical criticism that could, at last, define in a rigorously materialist way the exact link that binds history to the corporeal consciousness of the writer. Richard's criticism is, in its present state, ahistorical, but it is not *against* history; it sets history aside for the moment. For this reason, its incompleteness seems much more fertile to me than that of historicizing criticism which, however correct and useful its general schemas might be, and even if it manages to explain movements, groups, schools and systems, never manages to account for individual creation, except by resorting to the magical notion of genius.

To infer literature from history, we must, whether we like it or not, take a path through the particular object that is a writer's works. The importance of *Littérature et sensation* lies in exploring a number of embodied consciousnesses, in defining, in some precise cases, the structure of these object-works and thus in placing certain writers' imaginations within the reach of history. Richard makes historical criticism possible because he sets in place a criticism based on mediations. His analyses already enable us to glimpse, on their own terrain, a new broadening of the historical vision: for example, rudiments of a common existential consciousness appear at the same time in a number of contemporaries, such as Destutt de Tracy, Stendhal and Maine de Biran, enabling us to infer collective moods and historical types of sensations from these isolated analyses. It will be a great critical achievement to expand the notion of historical material and no longer reduce literature to a juxtaposition of concepts or political choices but, rather, historify the writer's very consciousness and the time of the act whereby a particular human body created literature. The day that is done, total historical criticism will owe a great deal to Jean-Pierre Richard.

Esprit (November 1955)

New Problems of Realism

Oeuvres complètes, Volume 1, pp. 656–9

This is the text of a paper delivered by Barthes to the third Franco-German authors' conference organized by the journal *Documents*. It was held at Vézelay in 1956 and devoted to the subject of literary realism. Like 'Brief Sociology', this piece was published in French by *Documents* (in July 1956), while a German translation appeared in the journal *Akzente: Zeitschrift für Dichtung* 3(4) (1956). Other writers attending the conference—fourteen were German and eight French—included Alain Robbe-Grillet, Paul Celan, Günther Eich, Walter Höllerer, Ilse Aichinger, Karl Korn and Luc Estang. Robbe-Grillet's own remarks on realism from the event were published as 'Une voie pour le roman futur' (A Future for the Novel), which became the second chapter of his programmatic work *Pour un nouveau roman*, published by Éditions de Minuit in 1963.

Underlying the notion of realism, as understood in our literature, is a remarkable paradox—the relations between writers and the real have, in fact, always been ethical rather than technical. *Historically speaking, realism is a moral idea.*

BOURGEOIS REALISM

1. Under a bourgeois regime, relations between the writer and society are ambiguous—under cover of liberalism, the bourgeois class *deputes* the writer to perform tasks of ideological justification. This is why bourgeois literature is *normally* idealist; it *chooses* from the mass of reality only that which is able to justify its idealist claims. It is a *selective* literature which arranges the real so as to provide only a reassuring image of it.

2. However, bourgeois writers have been known to rebel against the bourgeoisie and it is precisely in a subversive adjustment of the real that such rebellion finds expression. By *disrupting* the image the bourgeoisie wished to give of the real, the rebellious writer is carrying out a moral act—he is

spectacularly breaking the contract that bound him to the bourgeois class. In nineteenth-century France, all the literary trials to which the bourgeoisie subjected its writers (Baudelaire, Flaubert, [Emile] Zola) were trials of realism. They were, in other words, legal actions brought by the bourgeoisie against breaches of the ideological contract.

3. Subversion leads rebellious writers to declare real precisely those things the bourgeoisie is striving to hide. In that case, the real is *what is taboo* (sexuality, social deprivation). But since there is a choice here, and an elevation of things that were left outside literature, we may say that bourgeois realism is an inverted bourgeois idealism. This intensely moral structure of bourgeois realism is concealed, among its practitioners, behind the general alibi of objectivity, the real being described scientifically or in documentary fashion (the Naturalist school).

SOCIALIST REALISM

1. Socialist realism is a product of the specifically Marxist transformation of morality into politics (in the broadest sense of the term). To understand socialist realism, we have always to come back to the crucial celebration of Balzac by Marx and Engels (see in particular Engels, 'Letter to Miss Harkness', April 1888). Balzac is a realist because

he grasped human relations as relations that were, in the last instance, political. There is a new idea in this that wasn't present, for example, in Zola and it is a decisive one—the idea of structure. Realism is the art that grasps the deep structure of a society. To grasp the structure means to discern what is important (typical) and to reject the insignificant—*the real is what is significant*. Realism is the art of *correct* significations.

2. But what can confirm the *correctness* of a signification? The answer will be history and revolutionary praxis. However, the very idea of *correctness* contains a danger of morality—there is a great threat of socialist realism becoming a moral art once again, an art meant to *reassure* its new readers (as bourgeois idealism once did). Marx and Engels foresaw this danger clearly; they condemned it in advance as *tendentious literature* ('The more the author's [political] views are concealed, the better for the work of art,' Engels, 'Letter to Minna Kautsky', 1885[1]). Socialist realism is opposed to tendentious literature, even when it is socialist. In short, for socialist realism the real is qualitative; realism is selective and its object is signification.

---

1 This appears to be a misattribution. The phrase seems also to be from Engels' letter to Margaret Harkness of 1888. [Trans.]

1. Balzac's is a deep realism, a realism of types and essences. But a whole area of the real escapes him, and that is its *surface*. In Balzac, all that we should think of today as phenomenology—for example, portraits, landscapes, dialogues, the narrative, in short, the very *continuity* of the real—is still handled traditionally, in a classical, idealist way.

2. After Balzac and Marx and Engels, it remained for socialist realism to concern itself with the surface of the real and to find the means seriously to *dishabituate* realist description from its bourgeois ways. But what we might crudely term Zdhanovism brutally halted that useful development, leaving socialist realism arrested at the infantile stage of tendentious literature. Every attempt to extend the political grasp of the real to the techniques of surface description and all efforts to de-condition bourgeois form (on the part of the avant-garde, for example) were lumped together and discredited under the derogatory heading of *formalism*. Hence the ambiguous, unevolved character of Stalinist realist literature which is progressive in intent, hyper-bourgeois in form and at once realist and academic.

3. However, *outside* socialist realism and in the bourgeois milieu, taking advantage of its liberal status, the phenomenological reading of the real was intensifying—there were efforts to arrive at a

surface realism, though shorn of any requirement to achieve a deep, political realism. A number of French writers turned their attention to the problems of surface realism by promoting the philosophical notion of the *contingency* of objects (Heidegger's *da-sein*). At issue here is the problem of the signification or non-signification of the *surface*, a problem that gained notoriety in France through the fashion for the notion of the *absurd*.

Let me mention here three literary endeavours that relate to the problem of signification: Surrealism, which has always tried to enhance the meaningfulness of objects (Aragon speaks of 'giving absurd places a meaning they did not know they had'); Existentialism which, by contrast, attempted to rarefy signification, to rediscover the absurd aspect of the object (see Sartre's *Nausea*); and, lastly, the work of the young French novelist Alain Robbe-Grillet, who is looking for a realism that goes beyond the opposition between absurd and non-absurd—between loss of meaning and its multiplication—and is attempting to found a purely constative literature.

What unites these endeavours is that, in the debate over realism, they have foregrounded the problem of the *focal distance* from the real. How should the writer establish the distance from which he views reality?

We find ourselves today faced with a realism broken into two pieces: there is a depth realism, which is socialistic in structure but bourgeois in form, and a surface realism, which is free in form but apolitical and therefore bourgeois in structure.

My personal feeling is that the major problem for our literature is to join these two pieces and arrive at a total realism. The way forward, as I see it, is to set out from socialist realism to endow the surface of the real with significations that are no longer bourgeois. However, to reach that point, writers will have to accustom themselves to *seeing* the surface with untrammelled eyes. It is at this point that the constative literatures can, for all their idealism, prove useful. The contingency of the object cannot in any way be an element of the ultimate realism, since realism is essentially signi-fication, but it is perhaps a transient myth that is necessary for awakening writers to a total socialist literature, that is to say, enabling them to free themselves completely from bourgeois descriptive norms without, for all that, giving up on endowing all levels of the real with correct significations.

Documents (July 1956)

Works of Mass Culture and Explication de Texte

Barthes was a major contributor to the early numbers of the journal *Communications*, initially the journal of the Centre for the Study of Mass Communications, a research centre formed within the École pratique des hautes études en sciences sociales on the initiative of Georges Friedmann. Barthes made three contributions to its first issue (including two book reviews) and wrote this piece for the second, together with another longer text on an audience research project on the theme of 'stars'. This article formed part of a section entitled 'Debate: *Education and Mass Culture*' which also had contributions from, among others, Friedmann and Claude Bremond.

Explication de texte is a highly formalized method of close critical reading that has had a privileged position in the French education system. It was much advocated by Gustave Lanson whose methods were widely regarded, by the mid twentieth century, as exerting a conservative, if not indeed reactionary, influence on French pedagogy.

Oeuvres complètes, Volume 2, pp. 199–201

If works of mass culture come one day to be taught in the classroom, they will inevitably come up against the exercise that is typical of traditional French teaching methods—the *explication de texte*. What might happen then, and what should happen?

We ought first to remind the reader what *explication de texte* consists in. It is an analysis carried out on an extremely restrictive object—the text, that is to say, a piece of language. *Explication de texte* is a critique of language; quite naturally, then, it involves a 'philological' commentary, intended to give a comprehensive explanation of the meaning of the words, and a rhetorical analysis, the aim of which is to identify the (Aristotelian) 'elements' of the story. It is—and this ought not to be forgotten—a very culture-specific exercise, rooted in a very particular style of teaching inherited, by and large, from the Jesuits. Evidence of this cultural specificity— we might almost say national specificity, given how French the exercise is—can be seen in the reluctance of foreign students to fall in with its spirit; indeed, they often accuse it of murdering texts by excessive 'dissection'. At the same time, we may note that other types of commentary exist, such as commentary at the lexical level, as in Heideggerian discourse. As it stands, we cannot be unequivocal about the value of *explication*. Though extremely fruitful when applied to classical works that have been constructed in accordance with its own norms (in which case it protects the student from the temptation to engage in wordy paraphrase), there is a danger of its becoming scholastic when modern works are subjected to its procedures. A page of [Jean] Giraudoux can be 'properly' explained by applying the norms of the classical teaching methods, but those same norms will extract nothing from a page of [Samuel] Beckett.

In this context, what is a work of mass culture (by which I mean a work written for mass distribution through the channels of mass communication)? It is often an extra-linguistic work (a visual one, for example) or, in any event, a work that mixes different codes (words, images and music). It is above all, by definition, a work that has no hallowed status, insofar as it is not something that has been anthologized, produced by a process of selection, and filtered through a culture and a history. Where classical works are concerned, the question of their value is already settled when they are set before the student. In this case, not only is that question not settled but it isn't even certain that it should be raised. The work of mass culture is perhaps fundamentally an *immediate* work or, in other words, one that lacks any ethical mediation—it is consumed that way; that is its purpose and its deep function in society as a whole, and it isn't clear that, in singling it out, one isn't 'missing the point'. Moreover, its structure probably differs from the classical works (of our modern West); works of mass culture (commercial films, hit songs, photo stories) draw openly on large-scale collective models. 'Themes' are very important here, so these works call for a very active thematic criticism that is capable of tracing webs of themes across infinitely varied works. Above all, however, the mass work is subject to a peculiar logic which differs from that of classical works (this has not yet been studied and it will be very important to do so)—the composition of the narrative depends on certain rules (or constraints) that are probably imposed by very strict imperatives of consumption. As an example of this, let us cite a blockbuster film that tells of a war between two groups of barbarians (among the Mongols). In the middle of the film, there is every indication—according to the false rationality of the narrative—that a peace treaty is going to be signed; at the same time, the aesthetic logic, which actually governs the course of the action, suggests that it will not be. The film cannot end after half an hour, nor can it end without the spectacle of a pitched battle; there will *necessarily*, then, be a twist in the tale (since the aesthetic constraint wins out over the rational) which in this case takes the form of a betrayal. Similarly, it is impossible in the work of mass culture to allot certain actions to certain (positive) roles. We might group all these constraints under the heading of the internal *pertinence* of the work—mass works are narrowly pertinent (which is why avant-garde works may be defined as *non-pertinent*).

We cannot prescribe in detail the changes that *explication de texte* would have to undergo if its application were to be transferred from classical to mass works. We can only lay down that, if such popular works one day came to be taught (a question on which we do not pronounce here), a great shift in attitude would have to be required of teachers (a shift which many of them are perhaps already making). Clearly it will be necessary, first of all, to de-sacralize the work in question and not attempt to treat it as a classical work in disguise. Critical notions such as originality will have to be revised. The notion of aesthetic 'pertinence' will also have to be accepted—that is to say, the notion of a formal logic internal to a large collective structure, even if it be a very 'commercial' one. These are the two technical rules of the new *explication de texte*. There are some other, more ethical ones. Precisely insofar as the new aesthetic is accepted with equanimity, problems of value will have to be faced straightforwardly—it must always be possible to criticize the mass work in terms of the major human themes of alienation and reification, since the work of mass culture (like any other) is never 'innocent'. On the other hand, the new *explication de texte* must enable us to use the mass work to explain their own times to students and enable them to understand a modernity which, until now, has too often fallen outside the scope of the education system.

Communications 2 (March 1963)

The Human Sciences
and the Works
of Lévi-Strauss

Oeuvres complètes, Volume 2, pp. 570–2

The following text introduces a section entitled 'Débats et combats' on the work of Claude Lévi-Strauss in Volume 19, Issue 6 of the celebrated *Annales* journal. The two texts introduced by this piece were 'Signification et position de l'oeuvre de Lévi-Strauss' by the Argentine-born French author Raphaël Pividal and 'Telstar et les Aborigènes, ou "la pensée sauvage"' by Edmund Leach, the leading British anthropologist, then a lecturer at the University of Cambridge.

At its foundation in 1929 by Marc Bloch and Lucien Febvre, the journal was called *Annales d'histoire économique et sociale*, but by the time Barthes wrote for it, it had undergone four name changes and become *Annales. Économies, Sociétés, Civilisations.*[1]

1 Since 1994, it has had a sixth: *Annales. Histoire, Sciences sociales.*

La Pensée sauvage was published some two years ago [1962] and the *Annales* journal has been eager since that date to be involved in the discussion that would inevitably develop around this important book. However, we did not wish to open a debate on the works of Claude Lévi-Strauss without having available to us a number of genuinely thoughtful contributions and not merely spur-of-the-moment reactions. This explains why we took—and are still taking—our time. The debate that is beginning today is to continue for at least two issues after this one.

*

The *Annales* has been concerned for the unity of the human sciences too long for it to be necessary to justify the reception given here to the thought of Claude Lévi-Strauss. Everyone can clearly see today— and the texts that follow will express it well enough— that that thought, though always applied very concretely to a body of ethnographic material, is of general significance: it is both a method and a philosophy, demonstrating precisely that any method takes a stand on the world, on humanity and on the relations between the two. In the work of Lévi-Strauss, historians, sociologists, psychologists and communication theorists find not only explicit references to their own disciplines but also a constant reflexion on the very nature of any form of human science.

The unity of the human sciences is, admittedly, a long-standing dream, but that dream is often a lazy one. Many who have dreamt it have confined themselves to its theoretical premises, calling repeatedly for a total 'sociology', but in practice conceiving this only as a combination of particular disciplines—this is what we might call the 'interdisciplinary' myth. Yet it is not clear that the unity of the human sciences can be achieved simply by bringing disciplines together; it can be effected only at a deep level, after the old research frameworks, which too often are merely pedagogical frameworks, have been overturned—or at least forgotten. Whatever the associated risks, it is a unity that can be achieved only by subjection; the absolute pre-eminence of ethnology—and, behind it, of linguistics—in the work of Lévi-Strauss is not a merely accidental starting point. It commits us to accepting the possibility of a somewhat tyrannical rearrangement of our human sciences—it will no longer be sufficient to believe in working peacefully together on our research; we shall increasingly have to make a decision about the two contending 'realms' that are, it seems, destined to remain in play: anthropology and history. It will be clear, then, that there is no artificiality and no modishness involved in the *Annales*—which has already on a number of occasions outlined certain interconnections between the historical sciences and the sciences of structure—opening its pages to such a debate.

The works of Lévi-Strauss seem to possess a cathartic quality—starting out from very concrete research, they force upon us a thorough questioning of the very language of our science or, in other words, of our reason. This no doubt explains their prestige, but also the silence they still encounter from the technicians of the human sciences. We initially wanted historians, sociologists, linguists and ethnologists to discuss *La Pensée sauvage* with us here, each from the standpoint of their own discipline, but, with the exception of the fine contribution by Edmund Leach, it has up to the present only been philosophers who have replied. We regard this not merely as a significant fact but also as a positive one. First, because the philosopher's view has that particular capacity to 'strip down' a body of writing in such a way as to show up its ideological implications—something which no researcher can honestly wish to ignore or misrepresent. Second, and most important, because, insofar as Lévi-Strauss' work challenges scientific reason itself, philosophical transcendence is, so to speak, the prime elevation from which to consider it. It will no doubt be appropriate, subsequently, to descend to more limited territories and confront the Lévi-Straussian 'system' (we would prefer to speak of 'discourse' or *logos* in the sense of 'spoken science') with material from the traditional disciplines, but, between that future moment and the reading we can make today of a body of work that is both concrete and general, the philosopher seems to be a necessary mediator. By *re-presenting* the work of Lévi-Strauss to us, the contributors to this series of articles, like ancient 'storytellers', are making that work part of what we might call the intellectual myth of our times, at a moment when those times know no other myth than that of science.

*

We have taken the decision to begin with a presentation of the works of Claude Lévi-Strauss—a presentation which its author, Raphaël Pividal, has attempted to make as straightforward as possible. This presentation is followed, in this very issue, by the contribution from Edmund Leach who discusses two particularly contentious points in *La Pensée sauvage*, the problems of binarism and the sacred. In future issues we shall provide the points of view of Jean-Claude Piguet ('Les conflits de l'analyse et de la dialectique' [The Conflicts between Analysis and Dialectic]), Jean-François Lyotard ('Les Indiens ne cueillent pas de fleurs' [Indians Don't Gather Flowers]) and Raphaël Pividal ('Peut-on acclimater *La Pensée sauvage*?' [Can *La Pensée sauvage* Be Established Here?]). In the spirit of this series of articles, we are eager that each of these texts (or the work of Claude Lévi-Strauss itself) should give rise in turn to new contributions—they will be welcomed in the *Annales*.

Annales (November–December 1964)

Mass Culture, High Culture

Issue 5 of *Communications*, entitled 'Higher Culture and Mass Culture', published the proceedings of the conference held at Royaumont, under the auspices of the École pratique des hautes études, on the theme of 'Intellectuals and Mass Culture'. Barthes's contribution is to be found on pp. 35–9.

Oeuvres complètes, Volume 2, pp. 707–10

After an introductory paper by Paul F. Lazarsfeld (Columbia University), there were contributions from historian Robert Mandrou (École pratique des hautes études), Edgar Morin (Centre national de la recherche scientifique), Michel Tardy (University of Strasbourg), Henri Dieuzeide (Institut Pédagogique National), Joffre Dumazedier (Centre national de la recherche scientifique), Barthes and Michel Philipot, the head of music programming at the Office de Radiodiffusion-Télévision Française, the French national broadcaster. The debates were rounded off with some 'Final Thoughts' from Georges Friedmann.

When compared with the earlier article on 'Works of Mass Culture and *Explication de Texte*', this piece seems more markedly structuralist, particularly in the contention that a 'high' and a 'low' culture reflect a necessary division.

I would like to present some brief thoughts on the formal aspect of the opposition ordinarily established between mass culture and high culture. It seems to me that it isn't sufficient to try to define each of these cultures by its content, or even to stress the interactions and transpositions affecting the respective cultures' works and audiences, but that we should go further and enquire into the phenomenon of opposition itself: What might the *division* that a society itself imposes on its culture mean for that society? Also, far from downplaying or 'dialecticizing' the opposition between the two cultures, I shall propose that we take this opposition literally—not as a theoretical but as a factual datum. Let us not try, then, to define its terms but stay with the opposition itself, insofar as it is, in a sense, *spoken* by our society. In this way, in keeping with the desire formulated by previous speakers, we shall avoid committing the sociologist to a debate over value or definitions.

The essential task, then, is to describe the consciousness the community may have of the opposition between mass culture and high culture, since, from our standpoint, that opposition—only ever being something spoken—is entirely coterminous with the consciousness we have of it. Where, concretely, is this opposition to be found? Four kinds of sources are to be envisaged:

1. INSTITUTIONS

What are the institutions, in the broad sense of the term, in which such an opposition is registered? At a first glance we may cite educational institutions, whose syllabuses are selective and deal only with a limited culture (whatever the efforts of teachers to expand the notion of classical culture); state cultural institutions, such as the Academies, which are intended, by definition, to work to protect a certain form of culture and, hence, of secession; and state-administered mass communications (television and radio), whose schedules, though representing the entire cultural spectrum, make regular discriminations (if only in terms of their scheduling) between 'cultural' and 'popular' programmes. In this regard, it would be instructive to establish whether the private organs of mass communication don't have a much more syncretic conception of culture and whether the opposition isn't, therefore, increasingly peculiar to the state sector (at least in France). To these official institutions we may add all the elements of our civilization or *mores* that bear witness to a division within culture: art-house cinemas as opposed to the 'others', specialized publishing houses (outside of knowledge-based criteria), the cultural geography of towns and cities, tourist programmes, the activities of youth groups, etc.

2. EVIDENCE FROM THE PUBLIC

On this point we should need to assemble a highly varied documentation, including press articles, letters from consumers and interviews with them. Two problems arise here. We must first locate the awareness of opposition, with its varying degrees of intensity, in terms of the ordinary criteria of sociology (age, sex, occupation, geographical origin, educational background), then observe and structure the language in which the awareness of opposition is expressed. That language may very well articulate two types of judgement, implying two orders of value and hence two cultures, without ever naming or defining them. Adjectives like *boring, abstract, intellectual, serious* on the one hand and *vulgar, stupid, trivial* on the other seem to delimit two fields which may be highly changeable in content, as has often been pointed out, but which reveal an obvious functional antagonism (it is predicates that make for opposition, not subjects). A good structural analysis of the recorded corpus would surely provide interesting information on the lexicon of the opposition and, consequently, on its ideology, since the structure of lexicons always has a symbolic value.

3. EVIDENCE FROM THE 'CREATORS' AND 'DISTRIBUTORS' OF CULTURE

As a consumer good, the cultural work is 'weighed up' by those who produce it or put it into circulation as a function of certain criteria; at every moment in the preparation of a (radio or television) schedule and with every manuscript submitted to a publisher, these criteria of 'cultural self-interest' play their part. It would be useful to know (i) whether the 'values' of the creators and distributors form themselves into a simple opposition; and (ii) whether they are expressed in the same terms as those of the audiences at which the works are aimed.

4. WORKS OF CULTURAL SOCIOLOGY

At this point, a corpus of all the meta-languages attesting to the *mass culture–high culture* opposition should be assembled (if only that of our conference itself) and that corpus should be subjected to the linguistic analysis I've already referred to.

These are some fields in which we may hope to observe the opposition. If this exploration bore witness to the existence in the collective consciousness (that is to say, once again, in social parlances) of a cultural division, apprehended as a naked phenomenon, then it would be impossible not to be put in mind of two other major anthropological divisions that have recently been analysed in new terms. The first, within so-called primitive societies, is the division that ranges shamanic rites, behaviour and values—grouped around the 'medicine man'—against the 'normal' community that institutionally consigns everything anomic, subversive, aberrant or deviant within itself to the singularity of a role. This phenomenon has been described by Claude Lévi-Strauss in his *Introduction to the Work of Marcel Mauss*. The second division, within historical society, is the one between madness and reason, and hence between mad and 'sane' human beings. Michel Foucault, who has described this phenomenon over the course of three centuries of Western history, has shown that the division between reason and unreason was constant but that its contents were readily changeable.

In no way do I wish to equate, *at the level of content*, the opposition between mass culture and high culture as we experience it today with these divisions relating to magic or mental health. I would simply ask that we examine whether we aren't, here again, in the presence of a major adversative form of an anthropological kind that ought to be grasped in its very 'emptiness'. The most formal version of the opposition (the oppositions, we should say, since we have just suggested two others) would, at the species level, be the *minority–majority* paradigm. It seems that even the most cohesive societies are constantly setting this opposition back in place while filling it with very different, if not indeed contradictory, contents and displacing it, in a tireless process of reconstruction, to where technical, political and ideological advances still offer it a possible home. We may predict, then, that if the *mass culture–high culture* opposition one day passes away (there are some warning signs that it will), it will inevitably be replaced by a new mythic opposition, such as that between *technical and leisure culture* (this isn't a prediction, merely an example).

On the one hand, the changeability and confusion of contents, on the other, the permanence of the division—there is nothing mysterious about this law. The *dissymmetrical antithesis*, as represented in the eternal interplay between majority and minority, provides, as we are just beginning to see, the elementary dynamism of signification. There is no meaning where there isn't a minimal opposition between two irreversible terms (of the type *marked–unmarked*, for example). Thanks to the division into two cultures, the one a minority affair, the other belonging to the majority, our society is simply equipping itself with an intelligible culture—division is the formal condition for all culture once it leaves the level of techniques and moves onto the level of symbols.

Communications 5 (May 1965)

Response to a Survey
on Structuralism

*Oeuvres
complètes,
Volume 2,
pp. 715–17*

The following text did not appear in French until its publication in Barthes's *Oeuvres complètes*. On his copy of the Italian version, Barthes wrote: 'Published in 1965, written a long time ago'.

The word *structuralism* is beset by confusion. Recently, a thesis at the Sorbonne on structuralist methods in the social sciences included in these a large slice of American sociology, [Sigmund] Freud, the phenomenology of [Maurice] Merleau-Ponty, Gestalt theory, [Jean] Piaget's genetic epistemology, the criticism of [Lucien] Goldmann, Lévi-Strauss' anthropology and, of course, economics, on the grounds that, in all this research, the whole is posited from the outset as something other than the mere sum of its parts. As I see it (and I believe this standpoint is increasingly gaining ground in France under the influence of Lévi-Strauss), the word structuralism has a much more limited meaning—in my view, it refers to any systematic research that has a semantic frame of reference and is inspired by the linguistic model.

The reference to [Ferdinand] Saussure takes us into an even more particular form of structuralism or, if you prefer, a more responsible form. It is well known that a whole swathe of American linguistics, though structural, is not Saussurean in inspiration. Recourse to Saussureanism implies quite distinctively that the decision has been made not to limit systems of signification to their signifiers alone but to include the study of the signifieds themselves. This is an important decision, since, if we move on to connoted systems (of which literature is one), the signifieds form nothing less than the ideology of the society using the system. For a Saussurean, ideology is, therefore, part of semiology, as the set of connotative signifieds—it is perhaps easier for the Saussurean than for anyone else to envisage the synthesis of structures and history.

Once structuralism is defined in this way, the literary criticism that seeks to take its inspiration from it is faced with an enormous task. The principle of such a criticism is to regard the literary work (or a group of works, a *corpus*) as a signifying system. However, as this system itself is 'underpinned' by a first informational ensemble, which is articulated language (for English speakers, the English language), we are dealing with a variety of meta-language which we may, with [Louis] Hjelmslev, call *connotation*. Connotative semiotics has not been much studied as yet. Which are the connotative signifiers? How far do they extend? What system do they form? Are they discontinuous? To what signifieds do they refer? How are those signifieds organized among themselves (that is to say, what is their 'form')? Put with a deliberate naivety that subsequent research will doubtless overcome, these are the first questions a semiology of literature encounters on its path.

Reducing literature to a code (to speak crudely) in no way eliminates the historical problem but forces us, naturally, to think history in a new way. Admittedly, every structural analysis tends artificially to create synchronies and thereby always seems to bring history more or less to a standstill. But that is just a first moment of structuralism; a diachronic structuralism is possible and we are, in fact, currently seeing its beginnings in linguistics. Though the use of a code may last a very long time, codes are nonetheless historical— they are born, prevail and die in obedience to forces that are as yet unknown and are perhaps something like a new 'secret of history'. The code of our medicine, for example, which we call today 'clinical medicine', dates only from the beginning of the nineteenth century, as Foucault has demonstrated. Where literature is concerned, the connotative signifiers have been stable for more than a millennium; they have formed what has been called *rhetoric*, the entirely codified 'figures' of which governed literary signification from Antiquity to the nineteenth century (at least in France). However, it seems that a great change occurred towards the end of the nineteenth century— some figures (elements of the code) disappeared and others came into being; the rhetorical code was transformed and with it, of course, the whole 'ideology' of literature. It is these kinds of phenomena that a criticism which is both structural and historic ought to study. By revealing the stable and perishable character of codes of writing, it will obviously bring to light unforeseen periodizations and it will have to invent a new way of dividing up historical time or, in other words, a new understanding of history. Marxism has succeeded, by and large, in revealing the relationship between social history and ideological contents. With [György] Lukács and [Bertolt] Brecht it has even come close to a certain idea of form, as given through genre (novel, epic, tragedy). But literary language still remains a mystery to it and it is precisely for that reason that a new criticism has become historically necessary.

Catalogo Generale *Il Saggiatore 1958–1965*
(Mondadori, 1965)

A Dialectical Writing Practice

The eminent French philosopher and sociologist Edgar Morin was a colleague of Barthes's at the Centre for the Study of Mass Communications which became the Centre for Transdisciplinary Studies (Sociology, Anthropology, Semiology) and later, from 2007 onwards, The Edgar Morin Centre. Alongside Barthes, Georges Friedmann, Claude Bremond and Violette Morin, he was one of the early editors of *Communications*. In 1962, he published one of the earliest indepth studies of mass culture in French, *L'esprit du temps* (Paris: Grasset), which one reviewer described as 'a new and remarkable ethnology of the Man of the industrial societies of the second half of the twentieth century.'

Oeuvres complètes, Volume 2, pp. 718–19

When I read Edgar Morin, what wins me over each time is what I shall call his dialectical imagination. His work is dialectical on three levels: by its origins and references (Hegel and Marx); by its aim, which is always to find in the world, in the object the world offers for analysis, all the contradictory forces of history, of a genuinely total history, since Morin treats the future as a natural dimension of time; and by its structure. Though purely intellectual, Morin's work is nonetheless imaginary or, rather (to avoid any ambiguity), *imaginative*—it *sees* ideas, not separately or as classified culturally or tied to other ideas or phenomena, but as a kind of nomadic substance for which, from one end to the other (from Freud to Marx, and from revolution to science), books provide an enormous territory of migration. And while being forward-looking and syncretic, that imagination remains critical; it sees with equal force what is, what should not be and what ought to be. 'The principle of synthesis,' says Morin, 'in no sense extinguishes the principle of antagonism.' Nothing sums up better the challenge Morin faces up to throughout his analyses.

This challenge is not easy. It is less easy today than it was yesterday in the days of [Louis de] Bonald, [Charles] Fourier or [Jules] Michelet, because the dialectic imposes infinitely more severe demands than utopia. Against dialectical development, against the vision of contraries, movements and simultaneities, language puts up a natural resistance, because language is linear and monodic. Though the real is *several things at the same time*, language is condemned to say them one after the other. Analysis is its domain, not synthesis or antagonism. A writer can announce the dialectic but he cannot represent it. Morin is constantly engaged in this squaring of the circle. His writing, which is both direct and baroque, vigorous and mannered, situated outside literature and within rhetoric, seeks to impose on language what it is most loath to accept—a dialectical dimension.

How does it do this? First, by displacing the problems identified by raising them to an unexpected level. As soon as an antinomy threatens to solidify, Morin shifts it 'elsewhere', provides new terms to surround it and modify the system of which it was part. Morin follows to the letter Marx's precept (I'm quoting from memory) that 'History solves the old questions only by setting itself new ones.' In this way, he effects a real broadening of meaning. This isn't a metaphor. We know now that a sign is only effective if it can be integrated into a higher-order ensemble—words are words only because they exist in and through sentences. For the 'words' Morin's times provide him with, in an inevitably fragmentary, heteroclite way, he always tries to imagine a 'sentence' or, in other words, a wider horizon that establishes a meaning.

This, for Morin, is what gives dialectical discourse its impetus. But this movement is maintained at the level of the writing: a thing is never presented without its contradictory attributes, a fact is only ever defined as the—falsely symmetrical—*crossing* of a number of terms (the 'chiasmus' of old). Rhetoric here becomes a genuine dialectical instrument because in reality only form can, in the last instance, correct language's impotence to bring order to its movement, its contrariness and, generally, its *other* logic. The gongorism of Edgar Morin, like the gongorism of Luis de Góngora, is ultimately, then, the expression of a serious struggle, the stakes of which are ordinarily masked by the flatness of classical taste or the unhealthy ablutionism of the language purists. A writer is, admittedly, doomed never to produce anything concrete; but, by *choosing* the way he speaks, he can come close, through fascination, to what reality accomplishes through construction. This is what happens with Morin's writing. By setting out in a thousand ways the contrary aspects and future dimensions of phenomena, it eventually drives home the need for a dialectical approach. As a result, when you have read Morin, it is no longer possible to see things from just one side. Or, at least, if you persist in doing so, you do so with a sense of regret.

Combat (5 July 1965)

Interview on Structuralism

Oeuvres complètes, Volume 2, pp. 882–6

In the following piece, Barthes is being interviewed for the journal *Aletheia* 4 (May 1966) by Danielle Cohen, Jean-Claude Quirin, Dan Sperber and Serge Thion on the occasion of the publication of the French edition of *Elements of Semiology*.

'Éléments de sémiologie' was first published in *Communications* 4 (1964): 91–135, an issue which also contained Barthes's 'Rhétorique de l'image'. It was reprinted in a single volume with *Le degré zero de l'écriture* in 1965 in Éditions Gonthier's Médiations series. In that series, edited by Jean-Louis Ferrier, Gonthier also published such works as Lukács's *Theory of the Novel*, Pierre Francastel's *La réalité figurative* and Friedmann's *Sept études sur l'homme et la technique*.

English translations by Annette Lavers and Colin Smith of *Elements of Semiology* and *Writing Degree Zero* were published in separate volumes by Jonathan Cape of London in 1967. They have since been reissued in a single volume (London: Vintage, 2010).

ALETHEIA. Semiology has just been given its *Elements*.[1] To get to the heart of your concerns, perhaps it would be useful to ask about the nature of the project *Elements of Semiology* is part of.

ROLAND BARTHES. At very best, *Elements* is a provisional terminological synthesis, produced for didactic purposes as part of a project we can discuss. Saussure did in fact conceive and name a study of sign-systems in social life—semiology. He explored one of those systems, language. But when serious study of the other sectors of semiology was begun, there was a surprise in store—it isn't at all certain that,

---

1 The Centre for Mass Communications Studies devoted a recent issue of the journal *Communications* to semiological research, including in particular an important text by Roland Barthes entitled *Éléments de sémiologie* (*Elements of Semiology*), followed by a critical bibliography. See *Communications* 4 (November 1964): 31–144. That text, alongside *Le Degré zero de l'écriture* (*Writing Degree Zero*), has just been published in paperback.

in the social life of our times, there are sign systems of any great scope other than human language. If we confine ourselves to pure semiological systems, the only ones it's been possible to isolate turn out to be weak. The highway code, which is always cited, is an illustration of this.

Similarly, taking fashion as my object of study a few years ago, I quickly came to see that the real vestimentary system was very weak.[2] On the other hand, it's always accompanied by a system of representations that is, for its part, extremely rich in content. To begin with, clothing does indeed constitute a system of signs, an articulated set of signifiers, but it's never more than rudimentary and involves few signifieds. These non-linguistic systems are weak, which isn't surprising, since we give language the task of taking them over and producing poetics, ideologies and imaginaries out

---

2 See 'Le bleu est à la mode cette année. Note sur la recherche des unités signifiantes dans le vêtement de mode' (Blue Is in Fashion This Year. Note on Signifying Units in Fashionable Wear) in *Oeuvres complètes, Volume 1, 1942–1961* (Paris: Éditions du Seuil, 2002), pp. 1023–56; and *Système de la Mode* (Paris: Éditions du Seuil, 1967), available in English as *The Fashion System* (Matthew Ward and Richard Howard trans) (New York : Farrar Straus & Giroux, 1983).

of them. It's at the point where language takes up the baton that what's properly called fashion appears. It comes in already at the level of nomenclature, but it really makes itself felt in the development of a genuine rhetoric that we see deployed in fashion writing. Fashion in clothing comes intermixed with language—it isn't a pure semiological system. And indeed, with the most interesting objects of study, it's this impurity that seems to have to be present. Such a finding causes us to deviate somewhat from the Saussurian semiological project. This study of substances intermixed with language is something we might term translinguistics.

ALETHEIA. How does this takeover of a pure semiological system by language come about?

BARTHES. At the level of production, our society is subject to a calculating, accounting mentality. But between the real wear and tear to garments, which should determine new purchases according to economic calculation, and actual purchases (which happen more quickly than the rhythm of wear would suggest), another field intrudes itself— the field of fashion. This field of representation is governed by writing on fashion. Let us say that between economic rationality and actual behaviour—which is, strictly speaking, irrational— there is mediation by the instruments of mass communication. The fashion magazine, for example, mobilizes, by way of a stylistics, a rationality that is intended to compensate for the 'idleness' of the sign. In this sense, the gap between the two defines an ideology that has rhetoric as its form.

ALETHEIA. Someone like Betty Friedan has a quite different reading of advertising. She puts the emphasis on the economic decisions that govern the world of fashion. And when she moves from the sender to the receivers, it's social psychology she calls on to account for the fascinations and attractions of advertising. There seems here to be a self-contained loop that leaves no room for a semiology or a translinguistics applied to advertising.

BARTHES. We have to sort things out here, and to sort things out from a Saussurian standpoint is to separate *langue* (language) from *parole* (speech). Decisions about messages are of the order of speech, of *parole*. But that *parole* itself implies a language which we have to describe. This is why a trans-sociological position is possible. It will involve describing and analysing these intermediate worlds of connotation, these frozen syntagms as Saussure called them, these sub-codes, these idiolects which themselves end up forming a *langue*.

It's precisely the case that, as we move closer to *parole*, the world with its economic and other laws impinges on how things are said. The problem we have before us is the one Aristotle faced in his *Rhetoric*: How are we to code the larger units of *parole*? It might even be said that this problem arose before the problem of coding *langue*.

ALETHEIA. You study the rhetoric of the advertising image from such a standpoint.[3] But can you be certain of getting to the codes without ever referring to their function—economic persuasion?

BARTHES. It's quite right that the economic system imposes constraints on the semiotic system, but those constraints either intervene by determining impossibilities, in which case they simply mark the limits of the system, or they're creative, in which case they're incorporated as signifiers. It's true that the object is put into circulation by the infrastructure, but there isn't any mimetic relation, for example, between the structure of the novel and the economic structure. Fashion is clearly a privileged object, since it would be absurd to postulate a mimetic relation in this case.

ALETHEIA. To isolate one level of study methodologically is to deprive oneself of the means to understand the real constitution of the object. In the case of language no consequences ensue, since

---

3 See Roland Barthes, 'The Rhetoric of the Image' in *The Responsibility of Forms: Critical Essays on Music, Art and Representation* (Richard Howard trans.) (Berkeley: University of California Press, 1991), pp. 1–17.

ROLAND BARTHES

its function is obviously one of communication. But it isn't the same with fashion. Fashion isn't primarily communication—or perhaps it is communication but only secondarily.

BARTHES. You're trying to place yourself at a point where objects are improvised, natural. Yet that is to destroy the social. As soon as there is naming, the process of meaning begins.

ALETHEIA. Admittedly, no object is without its signification. Yet it doesn't follow that signifying is always its function. And looking for a function doesn't mean getting back to some improbable naturalness of meaning. The function of clothing can't be reduced to protecting the body from cold. Take the psychoanalysis of clothing.

BARTHES. Psychoanalysis may well find a phallic signified. It may review a large number of signifiers of such a thing and build up a symbolics. Semiology has a quite different aim—it studies the mode of organization of these signifiers. The psychoanalytic approach isn't invalidated—room is made for it. The pertinence of semiological analysis leaves space for other pertinent considerations.

ALETHEIA. How does semiology specifically carve out its objects?

BARTHES. I take it you're referring to the decision by which the object of an analysis is distinguished from its neighbours (there's another form of 'carving-out' or 'cutting-up' [*découpage*] internal to the object, which is very important in semiology). First, it must be said that structuralism leads us to work on a new timescale, on longer time periods, for which Giambattista Vico provided what we might call the poetic notion. Rhetoric, for example, is a very long-term object (two and a half thousand years). A new historical timescale can lead us to conceive new objects. When it comes to the actual criterion for isolating the object, we can be guided initially by the unity of substance. But this remains a tricky question.

ALETHEIA. There's the same problem in lexicology— the difficulty lies in eliminating the non-pertinent semes in order to determine an homogeneous corpus. And how this is done is particularly important, because, with any other choice of corpus, the denotation–connotation relationship is partially transformed. In any event, the question about the possibility of a particular delimitation isn't a preliminary difficulty, but the potential conclusion of a description of this kind, since it's clear that a description is always a construction. What matters is its intelligibility effect.

BARTHES. For a novel, for example, the criteria will be: its written nature (the fact that we're dealing with a written work, not one narrated orally); the assembling of actions; and 'the injection of motivations' by which Georges Dumézil distinguishes the novel from the myth.

ALETHEIA. Once the object has been isolated in this way, how is the study conducted?

BARTHES. I'm working at the moment on Flaubert's short story 'Un Coeur simple' ['A Simple Heart', 1877]. I'm not looking at the problem of creation. I'm not looking for what is Flaubert's, but, if I may put it this way, for what in Flaubert belongs to Propp.[4] There are some good models for this literary anthropology in folk tale and myth. One of the phases of the work will consist, then, in comparing the structure of 'Un Coeur simple' with the structure of the folk tale.

ALETHEIA. Will you use Greimas' actantial analysis in your approach to the structure of the story?

BARTHES. I shall have to try to.

ALETHEIA. When that analysis is done there'll be a residue, a remainder, which is precisely Flaubert's 'Un Coeur simple'. Yet what was new in the structural approach was the refusal to leave a residue at the end of the analysis. Doesn't an analysis like the one you're carrying out fall foul of [Noam] Chomsky's criticism of the Saussurian models?

BARTHES. At the level of description one chooses, there isn't, by definition, any residue, since the exhaustiveness of the description is one of the

---

4 Vladimir Propp, the Russian philologist and author of *Morphology of the Folktale* (Austin: University of Texas Press, second revised edition, 1968). [Trans.]

epistemological rules of structuralism. The other levels are obviously 'residues' until one actually describes them. For Chomsky himself, the signified is currently a further 'residue' and that's no small matter, but when we have a structural semantics, that residue will disappear. We have to add to the levels of description—at that point, the small number of general laws linking the levels will emerge. This is what we're currently trying to do with 'grammar' and 'lexicon'.

ALETHEIA. There's a need to enquire into the meaning of the structuralist meta-language, into the bias towards treating 'everything as an object in general', as Merleau-Ponty put it.

BARTHES. Knowledge is a meta-language that is, consequently, always under threat of becoming an object-language in the grip of some other, future meta-language. That's a healthy threat. Knowledge, unlike 'science', can quickly become a fetish. Structuralism is currently helping to 'de-fetishize' old, or competing, forms of knowledge. It enables us, for example, to bid farewell to the burdensome superego of totality. But it will inevitably become fetishized itself one day (if it 'catches on'). The important thing is to refuse to inherit, which Husserl called dogmatism.

Aletheia (May 1966)

Linguistics
and Literature

The following piece was the editor's intro-duction to Issue 12 of the journal *Langages* (December 1968), subtitled *Linguistique et littérature*. That particular number included articles by, among others, Gérard Genette, Roman Jakobson, Mikhail Bakhtin, Tzvetan Todorov, Julia Kristeva and Nicolas Ruwet.

This was Barthes's first contribution to *Langages* (his academic writing continued to be published mainly in *Communications*), which he helped found in 1966, alongside Algirdas Greimas, Jean Dubois, Bernard Pottier and Bernard Quemada. Its avowed aim, expressed in its first editorial in 1966 (which opened with the words 'The study of language is a necessary dimension of cul-ture today') was to make available the fruits of linguistic science to practitioners in other fields, but to do so in a serious, scientific manner. Early numbers were devoted to such themes as 'Logic and Linguistics', 'Dis-course Analysis' and 'Language Pathology'.

Oeuvres complètes, Volume 3, pp. 52–9

Linguistics and literature—it seems quite natural today to bring the two together. Isn't it natural that the science of language should concern itself with something that is indisputably language—namely, the literary text? Isn't it natural that literature, a technique of certain forms of language, should turn towards the theory of language? Isn't it natural, at the point when language is becoming a major preoccupation of the human sciences, philosophical thinking and creative experience, that linguistics should cast its light on the science of literature, as it is doing on ethnology, psychoanalysis and cultural sociology? How could literature remain apart from this sphere of influence that has linguistics at its centre? Might we not even say that it should have been the first field to open itself to linguistics?

What seems natural today (at least one hopes so) did, however, have to be won. There was for a long time, and there probably still is, resistance to the encounter between linguistics and literature. That resistance has been related to the status of each of these disciplines in our modern society. On the one hand, for many years, at least in France, the literary work has mainly been of interest for its content. To postulate that it is essentially language (and to subsequently draw the consequences from this), even though it is a materially obvious fact, would have been taken as an act of formalist provocation and met with the opprobrium attaching, since the death of classical rhetoric, to any halfway sustained formal considerations. To define literature as 'a thing of language' would have been to offend against its human (and humanistic) value, and to deny or downplay both its realist force (protected by the social and, in some cases, the socialist alibi) and its poetic power (which allegedly depends on an 'intuitive', 'tangible' act of communication). As a result, we have for many years now seen the study of literature (in France) concede a minor part of the text, 'style' or 'the writer's language' to a marginal department of the science of languages—philology. Admittedly, during this same period, linguistics itself— particularly, historical, comparatist linguistics—never dreamt for a moment that 'content' could be part of language or that the science of the forms of enunciation had any rights whatever over 'ideas', 'feelings' and 'genres'. Indeed, linguistics itself subscribed entirely to the separatist image literature wished to give of itself. Being subject to a very strong scientific superego, it felt no entitlement to deal with literature, since, as it saw matters, literature was located largely outside language (in the social, historical and aesthetic realms).

For a meeting between the two disciplines to occur, they have therefore had to overcome their own natures [*se vaincre elles-mêmes*], particularly in France where they were assuredly the furthest apart. There is already a history to this coming together. Let us take a first look, here, at the main features of this development (though not necessarily its main stages).

For centuries there was, in fact, a very extensive discipline in the West that saw it as its role to deal with relations between the literary work and language—namely, rhetoric. But rhetoric, in whatever ways it developed, had no scientific or even analytical or critical aim. It was initially (among the Greeks) a technique for oratory, then in the Middle Ages an element of a vision of the world and of speech. Lastly, in the French Classical Age, though already moribund, it was a code or body of rules for overseeing the creation of literary works, not for providing an account of their structure. Rhetoric has always been, then, a very extensive construction of the relations between the 'real' and speech; its longevity—two thousand years—is a source of some amazement to the historian and, on both these grounds, it deservedly commands our interest. And then, over the course of the years, rhetoric has also given rise to notions, classifications and problems which modernity may turn to good effect, and already has done. Relative to a linguistic science of literature, the intuitions of rhetoric have often been profound—it saw the literary work as a genuine language object and, in elaborating a technique of composition, it necessarily prefigured a science of discourse. What has held it back, when seen from today's standpoint, has been its normative position—it produced codes of rules to be observed rather than analytical concepts.

It is not, then, on the basis of ancient rhetoric (condemned by the 'modern' mind as early as the sixteenth century) that a science of discourse (let us call the conjunction of linguistics and literature, very generally, by this name) has been able to come into being or, to remain guarded on the matter, that a demand has been generated for the existence of such a science. The linguistic breakthrough towards the literary text occurred, it seems, from the analysis of the poetic message which is apparently the most formal of all constructed languages (at least in our civilization, where the gnomic form has little currency). We know the role played by Jakobson in this offensive (not forgetting his earlier ties to the Russian Formalists, among whom creative preoccupations, rather than strictly scientific ones, were very strong—a not insignificant fact). From the French point of view, we have to add the activity of other linguists who have contributed concepts that have been exploited quite naturally in the study of discourse. Most notable among these are Hjelmslev, with 'form of content' and connotation, and [Émile] Benveniste, whose ideas on enunciation (in particular on the person) turned out to be very much akin to certain explorations made by writers themselves. For to this rudimentary account of an encounter, we should add—and this is an important point—the activity of a number of writers whose thinking and practice have amounted to genuine linguistic endeavour. Since [Stéphane] Mallarmé, whose astuteness with regard to literary language still seems unsurpassable today, writers as different as [Paul] Valéry, Lautréamont or [Raymond] Roussel have either underscored the verbal nature of the literary work or revolutionized the conditions of its *readability*, a typically semiological notion. In very different styles and on the basis of at times opposing ideologies, these various writers have foregrounded not the composition—as in the days of rhetoric—but, more radically, the very production of the literary text. The writers of the *Tel Quel* group are currently conducting practical and theoretical activity (the one by writing texts and the other by following the developments of linguistics) that is a response to the strivings of linguists towards literature and of literary critics towards language.

*

The studies presented here have a certain national unity to them. A number of foreign researchers have chosen to join us, not to mention the great initiators such as Roman Jakobson and Mikhail Bakhtin whose presence we particularly value; in the main, however, this is a French effort. We are aware that there are throughout the world many researchers working on the linguistic or logical analysis of literary texts and we hope to develop increasingly frequent and increasingly better-organized working contacts with them (mainly through congresses and conferences, some of which are already planned). However, the French situation has its own particular character, as we have indicated. Unlike what has happened in the Anglo-Saxon countries and in Eastern Europe, no formalism of any kind has been able to develop in literary studies. The French critical tradition is entirely, exclusively focussed on contents or, at a pinch, on genres—these latter being conceived as historical objects whose origins are to be looked into, not as formal objects whose structures are to be determined. For French researchers, the encounter with linguistics has, therefore, something liberating about it, and this is ultimately what unites them best. We are talking of a group of young scholars, who come mainly from the Centre national de la recherche scientifique and the École pratique des hautes études and are grouped together in the Centre d'étude des communications de masse [Centre for the Study of Mass Communications] and the 'Semio-linguistic Section' of the 'Social Anthropology Laboratory' of the Collège de France, led by A[lgirdas] J[ulien] Greimas. They form a team, not a school. And their contributions are essentially 'working papers' representing moments in a process of ongoing research which remains, in the current state of affairs, highly personal and, as a consequence, essentially diverse.

This diversity is not a stylistic or oratorical point, made to justify each researcher working in relative isolation; it is the fundamental expression of the current status of literary semiotics. That semiotics can only be constituted by a dialectical labour. It can only lay foundations by displacing other elements. It cannot deal with a concrete object (a particular text) without directly and in that same process enunciating a theory of meaning. It cannot bring literature and linguistics together without ultimately subverting the idea we have of literature and linguistics. Semiotic research is diverse because it has to represent several aspects and several directions of this foundational contestation at the same time. Its legitimate first inclination is to accept the categories it inherits from linguistics; then, by the weight of the analysis and the very direction in which it is pulling, to turn against those categories and undermine them, gradually coming in this way to revolutionize the intellectual landscape in which we habitually range the main objects of literary culture. We can observe this course of development (some aspects of which are represented here through the different contributions) in respect of three themes that are among the most important in literary semiotics.

The first of these themes is the linguistic model itself. Though all the research derives from this model (if only by borrowing part of its vocabulary), it is no one's aim to be unconditionally faithful to it. In fact, all researchers distance themselves from it to a greater or lesser extent. This is because the semiotician must bow to a twofold theoretical demand: on the one hand, he assumes that general forms exist, common to all systems of meaning and, in consequence, what is brought to light by linguistics must also be found, *mutatis mutandis*, at another level—that of the literary work, for example—since it is itself the product of a certain process of meaning; on the other hand, he knows that an ordered set of sentences (a discourse) isn't a mere stringing-together of sentences and hence that something new and original occurs when we pass from the sentence to the discourse, even though that something is unfailingly semiological. To rein in the tyranny (or limit the prestige) of the linguistic model is not, then, a mere act of conventional caution or distance; it is to point to the central area of research, to identify something which is unknown and yet to be discovered, to assert that something will both be dependent on and run counter to linguistics, to seek a genuinely dialectical outcome from the scientific heritage.

The second theme is that of literary genres. It seems very difficult to undertake research in literary semiotics without referring, at the outset, to genres recognized by the tradition, since one has to work on a text and there is no text that isn't dependent on a genre. Consequently, there will be contributions here relating to the poetic, dramatic and narrative genres (other genres, needless to say, will have to be studied in this same spirit). However, genre, though apparently a recognized entity, isn't presented here as an aesthetic category but, rather, as a *type of discourse*. This first shift is an important one; it will enable us to deal one day with certain written productions that don't fall into an acknowledged genre and yet indisputably constitute special, marked discourses, such as scientific discourse, didactic discourse, wisdom discourse, etc. In other words, the concept of 'discourse' is wider than that of 'genre' and should enable us to break down the institutional boundaries of literature. This is not all—genre inevitably implies from the beginning a kind of norm one is trying to get back to by analysis, even if this subsequently means assessing real texts in terms of how far they depart from it. That position isn't without its dangers. On the one hand, there are always consequences in postulating a kind of human normality (even a highly formal normality). This is clearly seen when the decision is made that the poetic is merely a divergence from 'everyday' language, which is to suppose a—both social and structural—hierarchy of codes and, consequently, a logocentrism—a philosophical position that has many consequences. On the other hand, to develop the analysis on the basis of a word (such as Poetry or Narrative) runs a risk of nominalism— the definition of the genre, though purely lexicographical, ends up being taken as a real datum; this can be clearly seen with the word 'structure', the 'rigorous' definition of which makes it possible to exclude from structuralism the totality of structuralists! All this means that the notion of *genre* is acceptable only if it is displaced, destroyed or jettisoned much as the stages of a rocket might be. This splitting of the analytic process is all the more judicious for that fact that there is, as we have seen, in the recourse to the linguistic model a very strong temptation towards universalism: Since there are universals of language, why wouldn't there be universals of poetry or narrative? It is probably too early to decide about this and, in the current state of research, the universalist assumption is a fertile one—genres are useful starting points. To preserve the freedom of the analysis, it will be enough—as is already done by most researchers—to situate the specificity of genre not in very general rules of composition, in macro-structures (as Aristotelian poetics does), but in elementary syntactic schemas: *repetition–expectation* for the poetic genre; *noun–verb* for the narrative. This way, genre is identified with a specific unit of discourse and that unit may very well be scattered into, or transit into, very diverse works that belong to different 'genres'; there may be 'narrative' in (even non-narrative) poems, 'poetic' aspects to a didactic presentation, (syllogistic) 'logic' in a narrative, etc. It is generally the task of semio-literary research to define types of discourse, not different types of works.

The third oppositional theme raised by the semiology of discourse is Text itself. As we mentioned at the beginning, various writings previously regarded as 'unreadable' (for example, Lautréamont, Roussel) have, with the backing of a number of writers, come to be accepted into literature. These writings, which cannot be classified in terms of the traditional norms, and even subvert the notions of poetry or narrative, can only —fully—be *texts*, complete facts of discourse, without possible reference to (psychological, realist) contents or (lyrical, aesthetic) forms. By their mere existence, these texts have introduced into the centuries-long succession of literary works a break or difference—the difference precisely between the readable and the unreadable. The *readability* of the literary work has therefore become—or is in the process of becoming— a category, doubtless a very extensive, majority one but a theoretically relative, historical, contestable category of written production. It is no longer possible then, in essence, to reduce literary discourse to a monovalent logic, to a linear syntagm. Writing, in the sense of *écriture* (which is coming to stand in opposition now to *literature*), implies new logics capable of accounting for both the ruptures it effects and the space it occupies, since, in certain cases, that writing is neither 'sequential' nor 'linear' and hence the linguistic model comes to seem of only distant relevance, with more mathematical models appearing to be called for.

*

These few disruptions present here in embryo within the presentation of highly concrete studies, differ greatly in the extent of their subversiveness, and the differences between them may be seen as genuine divergences between researchers who are, nonetheless, bound together by a common language: some are attempting to get around the psychological image of literature, others undermining the usual classification of literary works, and yet others challenging concepts that are considered indispensable to literature. The deep and, as it were, ultimate significance of literary semiotics doesn't, as I see it, lie in adding to linguistic science or literary criticism a new department nor in complying with the current myth of 'interdisciplinarity': it isn't about getting the disciplines to communicate, but changing them and displacing the image we have of linguistics and literature, to the point, if necessary, of relegating one or other to the rank of historically out-dated system—a change which, as it seems to me, is already well underway. It is in fact entirely possible that linguistics, fragmenting at the very moment of its coming to be recognized as the supreme model, should gradually come to be seen as a science linked histori-cally to a certain object which is itself historical—namely, the spoken word. But once we take the view that writing cannot be regarded as a mere 'transcrip-tion' of the spoken word (the necessary reference here is to the work of Jacques Derrida), linguistics, which has never drawn this distinction, is in danger of being swept away, or at least of being confined to the study of oral communication and not of inscriptions. And it is very possible too that literature, despite its survival in mass culture, will gradually be deprived—through the work of writers themselves—of its traditional status as a realist or expressive art, destroying itself and being reborn in the form of an *écriture* which will no longer be exclusively linked to the printed word but will be constituted by every labour and practice of inscription. The text will render linguistics outdated, just as linguistics is currently doing with the literary work. This means that, when taken together, the studies presented here, each of which is already a *moment* in relation to its neighbour, simply form in their turn the beginnings of a transformation in which the essentials of our culture are in play.

Langages 3(12) (December 1968)

Ten Reasons
to Write

This article initially appeared in Italian as 'Dieci ragioni per scrivere'. The French version, from which this translation is made, remained unpublished until it appeared in Barthes's *Oeuvres complètes* in 2002.

Oeuvres complètes, Volume 3, pp. 100–01

I

Writing being neither a normative nor a scientific activity, I cannot say *why* or *for what* one writes. I can only list the reasons for which I imagine that I write:

1. Out of a need for pleasure which, as we well know, isn't unrelated to erotic enchantment.

2. Because writing decentres speech, the individual and the person, and accomplishes a labour whose origins are indiscernible.

3. To put a 'gift' to good effect, to perform a distinctive activity, to make a difference.

4. To be recognized, gratified, loved, contested, taken note of.

5. To perform ideological or counter-ideological tasks.

6. To obey the injunctions of a secret typology, of a distribution of combatants, of a permanent *evaluation*.

7. To gratify friends and irritate enemies.

8. To contribute to fissuring our society's symbolic system.

9. To produce new meanings—in other words, new forces—to lay hold of things in a new way, to alter and undermine the thrall exerted by meanings.

10. Lastly, as emerges from the deliberate multiplicity and contradictoriness of these reasons, to confound the idea—the idol or fetish—of Sole Determination and Cause (in the sense both of causality and the 'good cause') and in this way lend substance to the idea that there is greater value in a pluralistic activity that has no causality, purpose or generality, like the text itself.

II

The *unreadable* or counter-readable is clearly not something that can be given full and entire form. One can neither describe it nor wish for it; it is simply the affirmation of a radical critique of the readable and its previous compromises. One is no more duty bound to describe the writing of tomorrow than Marx was to describe Communist society or Nietzsche the figure of the *Übermensch*. It is revolutionary because it is associated not with a different political regime but with 'another way of feeling, another way of thinking'.

Corriere della sera (29 May 1969)

A Problematic
of Meaning

Oeuvres complètes, Volume 3, pp. 507–26

The following article originates in a paper delivered to a group of teachers in the field of Initiation in Audio-Visual Culture, Centre régional de documentation pédagogique, Bordeaux, in 1970. The contributors to the debate which followed Barthes's presentation are identified within the French text only by initials. The piece was translated into Italian in 1998 under the title 'I regimi antropologici del senso' (The Anthropological Regimes of Meaning).

Problems of meaning have become a very live issue over the last ten years or so for several reasons, the main one being the quite extraordinary development of linguistics in the last three decades. In the nineteenth century, linguistic research, though very important, developed mainly in the area of historical and comparative linguistics. At the beginning of this [twentieth] century, in around 1915, Ferdinand Saussure historically re-cast the foundations of what we might call a linguistics of language, rather than a linguistics of languages—that is to say, a linguistics concerned with the function of *parole* [speech], not with any particular group of languages.

Saussurean linguistics was picked up and developed by, among others, the Dane Hjelmslev and the subject has quite recently taken a new turn with the work of the American Noam Chomsky. There has been a development or, more precisely, an extension of the methods of linguistic analysis, on the basis of the articulated language we speak, to all the other kinds of languages that exist in social life but do not have articulated language as their vehicle. In this way, we have begun to study messages or sets of messages made up of images using analytic concepts originating in linguistics, such as, for example, the still image in the case of photography or drawing and the moving image in that of cinema (we may also cite a number of studies currently being undertaken on the theatre). I shall leave aside the problem of painting or artistic drawing for the moment and the study of gesture which is not yet highly developed.

We give the name 'semiology' to this general science of signs that has gradually been developed out of linguistics. To tell the truth, it would be better to call it *semiotics* because the word *semiology* has already been taken by medical language (where it means the science of recognizing signs or symptoms).

It would, however, be very useful to have two words: we could use *semiotics* to refer to particular systems of messages. There would, as a result, be a *semiotics* of the still image, a *semiotics* of the cinematographic image and a *semiotics* of gesture, while *semiology* would be the name we gave to the general science that united all these various semiotics.

Among all these fields into which linguistics has been extended, I want to focus particularly on the extension of methods of structural analysis (*insofar as linguistics has been structural for some thirty years now*) to discourse; that is to say, to a set of words or propositions of a higher order than the sentence. Current linguistics is a science that ends at the boundaries of the sentence. The linguist never describes ensembles greater than a sentence, which is regarded as the material unit of spoken or written sequences.

The literary text has, of course, been subjected to methods of analysis that have varied over the centuries, from ancient rhetoric to more aesthetic or, conversely, more positivistic approaches. But a set of sentences that may be termed a discourse had never previously been studied from a properly semiotic point of view. Such work is now well under way. Naturally, the research in question is not well known to the general public, since it has not yet produced any really decisive theoretical works. It is going on in research centres in the form of doctoral theses; this is still rather preliminary research, but the approach is already quite a sound one.

Another extension, moving outward from the linguistic heartland, is everything we today call *structuralism*. The word *structure* is a very old one. It might be said that it has had little pertinence in the last hundred years, when all the sciences have been more or less structural, from architecture to biology and grammar. But I think we should currently reserve the name structuralism for a methodological movement that very much acknowledges its direct connection with linguistics. In my view, this would be the most precise criterion for a definition. Obviously, we encounter human sciences that are apparently very far removed from linguistics but which we now know we can approach with methods of analysis and operational concepts that derive from that subject. Moreover, the two most personalized, most distinctive, most characteristic structural research projects of the moment are, on the one hand, that of Lévi-Strauss in ethnology and anthropology and, on the other, that of Dr [Jacques] Lacan in psychoanalysis, who has brought together the world of the psyche and concepts from linguistics in an extremely evocative way, and postulated—to quote the phrase attributed to him—that the unconscious itself, seen from a psychoanalytic perspective, is structured like a language.

The objection is sometimes heard that this topicality of problems of meaning is ultimately a purely modish phenomenon. Some have even gone so far as to connect it with Gaullism, insofar as it seems, at first sight, to involve a set of methods which are apparently unconcerned with history and concrete or social matters and are merely formal or formalizing in appearance. The success of these methods has been seen as something of a mark of the de-politicization of intellectual research. This is an extremely crude contention—in my view, the current interest in the problems of meaning far exceeds mere topicality. It represents a groundswell within the civilization of the second half of the twentieth century.

Whereas, in the human sciences, the second half of the nineteenth century was dominated by the notion of *fact*—by the pursuit of and establishment of the *fact* and the dominance of the *fact*—research in the twentieth century is dominated by meaning. There is here a kind of very large-scale collective historical project that exceeds all of us and which means that we are currently, to some extent, seeing language in the deepest, most extensive sense of the term. Language is the continent to be explored, as though the planetary exploration of the cosmonauts had its counterpart, in terms of interiority, in the exploration of a very little-known territory which is precisely that of language or, if you will, signification, meaning.

Meaning is a general, imprecise word. But we can say that we know quite well what meaning is, following an extremely elementary schema to which we always have to return—*meaning is the union of a signifier and a signified*. The characteristics of both are quite well known, quite well classified—or that is, at least, the case with the signifier. What is less clear at this juncture is the signified.

Where does meaning begin and end? Ultimately, this is always where the problem lies. We can of course provide—ideological or aesthetic—solutions to the problem of the bounds of meaning, but a precise technical response is much more difficult.

It is absolutely obvious that a single signified can have several signifiers or a signifier several signifieds; this is what is properly called polysemy, a kind of inequality between the two terms, signifier and signified.

Currently in the linguistics of language a distinction is made between two essential areas: syntax and semantics (the meaning of words). The linguistics of syntax has developed and made surprising progress, especially in recent times in the work of Chomsky. But the establishment, the development of *structural semantics* is proving very difficult. There are some excellent semanticists (Greimas, for example), but it cannot be said that there currently exists a *structural semantics* as well founded as Chomsky's generative grammar, for example. It is clear that it is precisely the phenomenon of polysemy that has hampered the development of semantics in linguistic science. It is because polysemy exists that it is extremely difficult to study meaning properly so called. You can study relations—that is the job of syntax—but meanings themselves are very difficult to study. And at a more technical and operational, less speculative level, the progress of translating machines has also been slowed by this problem of polysemy. It is because polysemy exists that it is difficult to construct translating machines convincingly. And it is in order to encompass this formidable problem of polysemy that symbolic systems of interpretation are developed periodically. The latest of these, or, at least, the most important, has been psychoanalysis, a system of interpretation in the proper sense of the word, which attempts precisely to conceptualize and systematize polysemy. Psychoanalysis works on the fundamental assumption that certain phenomena have several meanings, or certain symptoms, in the psychical order, have several meanings—that is, that they are polysemic. By contrast, the—often burning— urgency of this problem of meaning, and particularly of polysemy, is attested by the fact that institutions or the *institution* itself—the social institution—always regard it as their/its task to keep watch over meaning, to keep watch over the proliferation of meanings. For example, the substantial development of mathematical formalization in the language of the human sciences is a means of countering the risks of polysemy. In another area, in the interpretation of literary texts, a kind of surveillance is also exercised by the institution—in this case, the University—over the freedom to interpret texts or, in other words, over the infinite polysemic character, so to speak, of a literary text. We can describe philology as just that science, allotted the role of monitoring the polysemic excesses that are part of the very nature of meaning. And if we look at meaning this way—that is to say, in its relations to the institution or to institutions—we see that it is in reality a very pressing issue: for centuries almost all the ideological battles of humanity—of Western humanity, at any rate—have been battles over meaning; it is always around an interpretation, be it in theology, sociology or, precisely, in philology, that the most intense polemics and even battles take place. It is in relation, then, to this problem of the bounds of sense that I would like to try to offer, in a broad and hence not very rigorous theoretical sweep, a kind of classification of what I shall term *the different anthropological regimes of meaning*.

They are three in number.

The first regime is that of *monosemy*, a social, institutional or aesthetic ideological system in which messages or signifiers are held to have a single meaning that is the right one. This monosemy—that is to say, the assumption that there is a single meaning—is a form of what pathologists of language call asymbolia.

It is a regime in which there is a sort of blindness or deafness to symbols. I use the word 'symbol' here in an extremely simple, broad sense—namely, to mean any coexistence between two meanings; where at least two meanings coexist there is a symbol. If, as a consequence, the assumption is made that there is only one meaning, this is to declare oneself, as it were, impervious, deaf or blind to symbols. It might be useful to remind the reader here that asymbolia is regarded by language specialists as a pathological trait. The fact of being deaf or impervious or blind to symbols is, as it were, the sign that something isn't right. Current efforts to situate the importance of this asymbolia in certain individuals from a psychoanalytic and psychosomatic standpoint have been relatively successful. The École de Psychosomatique in Paris has done some very interesting work which seems to show that psychosomatic patients are precisely people who do not symbolize within themselves, who are incapable of symbolizing—particularly of symbolizing their own bodies. As a consequence, they cannot say anything, they cannot speak and, furthermore, they cannot *fantasize.* The *fantasy* is the realm of the symbol. It appears to be because he doesn't fantasize that the sufferer experiences this form of psychosomatic disorder. The—paradoxical but obvious—consequence is that, in order to treat a psychosomatic patient, a way has to be found to restore the patient's ability to symbolize, to fantasize and to live within symbols. The way to cure the patients would seem to consist in giving them a neurosis, insofar as neurosis is precisely where symbols and fantasies hold sway.

The symbol is a strictly human phenomenon. Yet, the problem of animal language is a very fashionable one. However, after believing, in effect, that animals spoke, or at any rate had a language that we could reconstitute (this began with bees, was then extended to crows and jackdaws and subsequently to dolphins), we are not sure now that animal language exists. What is certain is that there is animal communication, but what distinguishes human beings fundamentally from animals in that area is that human beings are alone capable of symbolization. Asymbolia is thus a specifically human disorder. It is serious when it afflicts the individual along the psychosomatic path outlined above, but it would also be very serious at the civilizational level to arrive, through a kind of series of ruses of history, at a collective state of asymbolia. This is not the case with us, though mythological and mythic power are extremely well hidden in our technicist civilization. Thanks to television, the popular press, radio and films, there is a great churning of symbols in our society.

Obviously, we also come up against institutional forms of this monosemy in the form of all the disciplines—or, rather, all the languages—that assume, in a clearly very strict way, that a language, message or discourse (or a signifier) has only one meaning and, consequently, that there is a literal sense or a literalness of meaning to which we must cleave. In reality, though monosemy is useful in certain precise cases and though it is a mark of rigour and lucidity in certain types of language, more broadly and generally it entails some very serious disadvantages—among other things, a discourse that were entirely monosemic or asymbolic would ultimately be entirely tautological.

POLYSEMY

The regime of *polysemy* is the form of language, in the very broad sense of the term, of the societies that accept mythic language—that is to say, that accept what Hegel called 'the *frisson* of meaning'.[1] Hegel said

1 Barthes has already made this reference to Hegel's perception of a *frisson du sens* among the Greeks in an earlier essay ('L'activité structuraliste', *Oeuvres complètes, Volume 2, 1962–1967*, p. 471). However, the words in inverted commas appear not to be a direct quotation but a reference to a passage in Hegel's *Lectures on the Philosophy of History* where the notion of *frisson*

the ancient Greeks attributed multiple meanings to all natural and human phenomena: to woods, springs, forests and rivers. As a consequence, the whole of nature appeared to human beings—and appears to the mythic human being—as animated by a kind of frisson of meaning. The expression is a very fine one and it points precisely to this symbolic power, this polysemic power of societies—and particularly of mythic societies. The problem isn't to develop symbols—symbols are everywhere—but to accept them. Here, as examples, are three different forms of this polysemy. First, the archaic, ethnological version of polysemy or symbolism, as it were, of *symbolia* in the full sense of the term, which lies in all those mythical societies in which everything signifies [*est signifiant*]: nature, plants, animals, architecture, narratives, kinship relations. Meaning is everywhere and is acknowledged to be everywhere.

Second comes the regime of *hierarchized polysemy* or, in other words, the modes of thought which accept the idea that a sign has several meanings but think

[*schauer*] is intimately linked to the presence of the god Pan—'Pan ist der allgemeine Schauer in der Stille der Wälder'. See G. W. F. Hegel, *Vorlesungen über die Philosophie der Geschichte, Werke in zwanzig Bänden* (Frankfurt-am-Main: Suhrkamp Verlag, 1970), VOL. 12, p. 289. [Trans.]

that, among all these meanings, there is, all the same, one that is to be preferred and that is the true meaning. As an example we may cite the conception of meaning in medieval theology, particularly in Dante, a theory we find throughout the Middle Ages with regard to the Scriptures, an essential reality on which medieval man focussed his thinking. This conception was the theory of the four meanings. It was accepted by theology that the Gospels, the Scriptures in general or a parable or even a sentence from the Gospels always had four meanings at once: a literal meaning, the sense of the words themselves; then, behind this, a historical meaning relating to the humanity of Jesus; behind that, a moral meaning which involved ethics and man's duty; and, fourth, the most important, ultimate meaning—the deepest, most secret and most hidden, but also the vital meaning—the one termed anagogic because that was the meaning one found when one had gone through all the others.

A third possible form comes with the regimes of meaning that allow for interpretation, that grant a right to interpret the sign. This, then, is the form of polysemy that secular, rational societies grant themselves. A society like our own allows interpretation. It does not always allow it; sometimes it singularly limits the right to interpret a message, but let us say, all in all—if only because the word exists—that interpretation is a sort of secular, rational, limited recognition of the right to polysemy. This is, for example, what we find in the rights of literary criticism, when these are recognized. Similarly, there is certainly no way we can currently imagine a semiotics of the image that would not be a semiotics of polysemy. The image, of its very nature, constitutes a polysemic message. Images cannot be reduced to a single meaning and hence, in order to create a semiology of the image, we have first to recognize the polysemic power, constitution and nature of every image. And this is true of the image that seems, in theory, to be the most objective and most real—namely, photography. We know full well that photography is a polysemic message like the others.

ASEMIA

A third form of a regime of meaning would be a regime of asemia, that is to say, of absence of meaning or, more precisely, exemption from meaning. At the very general level we are working on here, asemia—that is to say, non-symbolia which is, as we shall see, different from asymbolia—can represent only a limit-experience and it is in the area of limit-experiences, at the level of societies and civilizations, that we have to interrogate it. Involved here are efforts, highly localized in certain civilizations or societies, to arrive at what I call a total exemption from meaning. This has nothing to do, structurally, with the absurd. The absurd or absurdity is a meaning—the meaning of the absurd. Hence exemption from meaning is an infinitely more difficult state of meaning to achieve; it is a kind of void of meaning or, rather, it is meaning felt and read as void, which is not the case with the absurd. Where can we find such a void of meaning in order to provide some examples of it? The answer is that all formalized languages—those of mathematics, in particular, or of logic—are languages empty of meaning. They are made up of pure relations, but there is no plenitude of meaning inserted within these relations. They might be seen as languages that exist only through their syntax and not through their lexicon. This is more or less what this void may be said to be, this empty language of formalized systems.

For another area far removed in space, if not in time, where we might come at the idea of an empty language or empty meaning, we might look to mystical experiences. But I shall add right away that it isn't among the descriptions of Christian mysticism—even though they play a great deal on this idea of the void and the sense of emptiness, on the idea of night (in such mystics as Saint John of the Cross or Teresa of Avila)—that I shall look for the best example but, rather, among experiences to be found in non-monotheistic religions, since monotheism has a very precise relationship with a certain use and conception of meaning—mono-meaning [*mono-sens*], if I may coin such a term. Monotheism doesn't provide a good example of this kind of total liberation from meaning and exemption from meaning that I'm trying to come at here. For this void and this exemption from meaning, we have to look, rather, to experiences such as those of Zen Buddhism (Japanese Buddhism). The whole of Zen asceticism is aimed precisely at a kind of emptying-out, of emptiness of meaning. And the theorists of Zen very well understood that the most difficult undertaking in the world is not to bestow meaning (we do this naturally) but to take it away. Hence it is this which has a certain value with regard to spiritual asceticism. There is, among other things, in Zen a meditation exercise (the Western words are unhelpful here, they are mere approximations) which is really a thoroughly impressive exercise in liberation from meaning—in it, the monk gives the aspiring meditator (another monk, perhaps, or lay people on retreat) what appears to be a wholly absurd phrase or anecdote. The meditation doesn't consist in ultimately finding a meaning in the absurd phrase but in using the absurdity of the phrase to experience emptiness of meaning. Lastly, there is, paradoxically, a third field in which we currently encounter this practice of exemption from meaning—a certain literary avant-garde. Currently, for example, the texts and thinking of a group like *Tel Quel* revolve round a kind of destruction of readability and of the readable.

We may insert here a definition of the readable; in the study of language, Chomsky distinguishes between grammatical sentences and ungrammatical ones.

A grammatical sentence must satisfy the syntactic rules and norms of a language. But that sentence, which is grammatical because it satisfies the rules of syntax, may, as Chomsky sees it, be entirely devoid of meaning. He has provided an example which is now rather famous: 'Colourless green ideas sleep furiously.' Here is a sentence that is entirely grammatical in English but entirely meaningless in Chomsky's view, and this leads him to make a further distinction between *grammatical sentences* and *non-interpretable sentences*. The quoted sentence is grammatical but it cannot be said to be interpretable. Chomsky has worked solely on grammatical sentences, leaving aside the problem of the meaning of the lexicon which, as we have pointed out, lags very far behind the problem of syntax.

Jakobson has responded to Chomsky with the contention that there is always, in reality, a point at which this sentence, which Chomsky declares meaningless, may have a meaning. This depends on context; and even if a sentence were to prove resistant to as many contexts as one might possibly imagine, there would always be a poetic context in which it could be interpretable again.

The problem gets interesting when transposed to the discursive level. What is a classical discourse in the very broad sense of the term—for example, a paragraph by Balzac or Stendhal or a stanza by Baudelaire or a paragraph by Camus or Homer? In all this literature, the sequences of sentences, and not just each individual sentence, have an interpretable character; it is this interpretable character of discourse that can be said to constitute the *readable* and, hence, it is precisely this *readability* which we regard, most of the time, as entirely universal and natural. It is this readability that is, to some degree, thrown into question by certain experiments on the part of the literary avant-garde which, by their very nature, involve texts that don't have this character of interpretability. The work of Lautréamont might be said to be an example of non-interpretable discourse, which would thereby represent for us the possibility of a discourse that is more or less unreadable in the proper sense of the term. Some very interesting thinking is going on within this avant-garde on readability and the limits of the readable. It is an experiment in asemia or in exploring a discourse that would in some way be unburdened of meaning—or, at any rate, of the old regime of meaning.

What is at stake in these various reflections or problems? It seems to me that we can already situate these problems of meaning at three levels. The first of these is the *psychological*. Here we have to refer once again to the work of Lacan. Lacan has described the human psyche as a field where chains of signifiers are elaborated, relays of signifiers, each signifier becoming the signified of another signifier which carries it further. It is chains of symbols, built in a kind of metaphorical form (since metaphor itself is a chain of signifiers), that might be said to structure, as it were, the unconscious and to have, at bottom, just one single ultimate signified. The psychical world as a whole can be seen as a world occupied by signifiers at all levels, with all these signifiers referring back, in the unconscious, to a single, ultimate signified which Lacan calls the *paternal metaphor*. However—and this is where Lacan has formulated things in a novel way—for Lacan, the ultimate signified, which is, in a sense, at the bottom or end of these chains of signifiers in the unconscious, is a lack, a void. It is, in psychoanalytic terms, the phallic lack, the phallus being the male sex regarded for its signifying value, regarded as symbol. And this phallic lack is linked to the basic castration complex that is, allegedly, at the bottom or end of these chains of signifiers, with our psyche, whether normal or pathological, spending its time elaborating symbols and signifiers out of a void—the void defined in psychoanalytic terms by castration. This is new and important precisely because it stands opposed to all the psychologies of plenitude, all the psychologies of essence and of psychological essences; this represents an extremely novel way of pondering the relations between meaning and emptiness.

A second level is the *metaphysical level* as we can see it explored currently by the texts of Derrida. Since Saussure, we have known, very distinctly, that the sign is a difference. For there to be sign, there has to be difference, a difference between two signifiers (paradigmatic play). Saussure was the first to say, in a very revolutionary way, that language was simply a system of differences. Derrida pushed these matters as far as they would go—he saw that the sign was a difference, that it was the beginning of a sort of infinite process which pushes the signified back *ad infinitum*. Up to now we thought we needed this kind of end-stop to meaning. We thought that signs were a mix of signifiers and signifieds but that once the signified was reached, the sign stopped there—everything was full, all was fulfilled, everything was normal. We are now beginning to see that sign systems can never come to a halt, that we can never stop these systems at ultimate signifieds or *an* ultimate signified. This is clearly the beginning of a metaphysical thinking of very great scope, which is also, in reality, profoundly atheistic, since theological systems make God the ultimate signified.

It would be difficult to conceive God as the signifier of something. God is what is signified—it is He who is at the bottom of everything as ultimate signified and it is He who is, so to speak, at the end of all the chains of symbols and signifying transformations. As soon as one asserts there is no ultimate signified and that signs are always infinitely deferred systems of differences, this is clearly a radical contesting of theology and also of the very notion of origin. It is a way of thinking or *unthinking* the origin since, in an infinite process of differences, the origin itself can no longer be thought.

Up to now, a structure was always conceived of as having a centre. Yet now, given the research pursued by such as Lacan, Lévi-Strauss and Derrida and the formulations they have arrived at, we are increasingly forced to attempt to think in terms of decentred structures and this is why language has become something very important. This is not at all for reasons of fashion or chance, but because language can be seen as the very exemplum of a decentred structure. In a dictionary, for example, it is a straightforward matter to piece together the structure of words or meanings among themselves, but you can only ever define a word with the help of other words. Hence it is, theoretically, a vertiginous object. If we don't treat it as such, this is for a purely contingent reason—we stop as soon as we reach the first sign that gives us a definition of the word. But if we really wanted to handle the dictionary theoretically for what it is, then we would have to look up the definition of every word that is used in defining another, and go on doing this indefinitely. As a result, we would never arrive at a point where the structure was really structured or centred.

Lastly, a third level of responsibility for all these problems is the one offered by that literary avant-garde I have spoken of. I shall refer to this as a *political level*. We may genuinely ask ourselves whether there isn't ultimately a kind of macro-historical relationship, at the level of very broad types of society or civilization, between a certain elaboration of meanings—of systems of meanings—and instruments of power or production, such as money. There is perhaps a sort of relation between meaning and money, a single conception indeed of value, of *being equivalent to*. It is a very remarkable phenomenon that terms which apply to the economy and currency also apply to language and, when Saussure wanted to find a comparison to explain what language was, he reached very innocently for economics as a source of metaphor.

Right now, if certain systems of signs in our consumer society that are centred on money were studied more closely, we would realize that there are close, organic relations between certain regimes of meaning and certain laws of consumption. This is to some extent what I was attempting to suggest in my studies of the language of fashion. In fashion, what actually sells are not so much the dream-like representations attached to forms of clothing, however much effort the fashion magazines exert in that direction. What actually constitutes fashion as an object of purchase is precisely that it is constructed as a system of signs. In fashion, it isn't dreams that sell, but meaning.

DISCUSSION

J. Out of a group of twenty-seven second-formers, two pupils, when given ten successive images, are incapable of 'fantasizing'. For example, if I present them with a horse in a meadow, they will say 'the horse is in the meadow' and so on, whereas the twenty-five other pupils behave differently. They say, 'It's a white horse,' etc.

BARTHES. I actually think that if there are only two out of twenty-five [*sic*], then you have a very good class, a class that's very good at symbolizing.

J. In other words, one can in fact attribute the phenomenon of monosemy to them . . .

BARTHES. Asymbolia. As it happens, I somewhat regret having presented things this way, because it lends credence to the idea that there's a norm and certain anomalies—a healthy state and disorders—which is always a little dangerous.

I believe the power of symbolization is one of the specific characteristics of human beings and, as a consequence, in relation to that anthropological fact, we can study a certain number of states, of phenomena, from the pedagogical viewpoint. I suppose this is your problem too—to manage to make students fantasize in front of images. Tautology is the fact that a=a. A tautological universe would be a horrible place to live and we sometimes have tautological reactions in us—faced with over-sophisticated arguments, we're sometimes tempted to respond that 'A cat's just a cat' or 'A penny's a penny,' etc. These are resistances to symbolization. Many instances of what we call 'common sense' can be interpreted as resistances to symbolization. There's a lot of aggressiveness in common sense, an aggressiveness that's often directed against symbols.

D. Don't you find, rather, that a lack of the ability to symbolize reveals a difficulty in translating one system of signs into another?

BARTHES. Roughly speaking, there are two main kinds of silence or aphasia: silences of censorship, which are very rich, very heavy silences, and then this silence of the psychosomatic individual, which has been defined a little more precisely in recent times. This is a much more terrible silence because it's really one in which 'there's nothing to be said': 'I'm not talking, not because I've too much to say and want to hide it, but because, really, I've nothing to say at the deepest level of my body—my body echoes with nothing, resonates with no sound when confronted with the phenomenon, the image.' A completely aphasic reaction would perhaps be better than a purely denotative one. If you say simply, 'There's a horse and a car there,' that would probably indicate a silence of phantasmatic incapability more than one of censorship. The question is whether the handling of language should always be interpreted from a psychoanalytic point of view or whether you can simply interpret it as an instrument. This is a very serious question, particularly for teachers, since in theory they're tasked with teaching how to handle this instrument. I'm inclined to think that it isn't just the instrument that you teach. If someone won't speak well or can't speak well, then that isn't just because of a lack of knowledge where the instrument's concerned.

MADEMOISELLE J. Do you personally think that it's possible to teach this aptitude to symbolize? And if so, to what extent?

BARTHES. I'm not entirely sure. I believe the first step in education is one of liberation. Images provide a wonderful terrain for freeing up symbolization a little. Then the trick is to lift the censorship, to unblock what's channelling meaning, what's channelling reading—to allow interpretations to proliferate to some degree. I believe that's true education. As ever, it's all about liberation in a sense.

MADEMOISELLE T. In teaching modern languages, for example, when an image is programmed to provide a determinate meaning, then, all things considered, it might be said to be negating that liberation.

BARTHES. I don't know. With the problem of the audiovisual, I think things are far from resolved— there are lots of things here that aren't well understood and perhaps not always clearly perceived even.

There's such a big gap between the image of a chair, however conceptual it may be, and the word 'chair'. On the one side, there's this whole area of arbitrariness and lack of 'motivation'. On the other, there's the image with its ambiguity, its relation of figuration of the referent and motivation by it.

MADEMOISELLE T. It seems that there's currently a fear that the symbol will disappear. Can't we see that fear in science-fiction films like *Alphaville* . . .

BARTHES. This is the problem of the fear of the mechanized, scientified world. I thought *Alphaville* was a very bad film. What I mean is that this ideology that consists in seeing technical progress as a backward ideological step annoys me. There's no reason why the fact of having fridges, washing machines or cars should be bad for symbols or the mind. If there is to be a consumer civilization, we have to organize it at the symbolic level, but it would be wrong to think that we have to go back a hundred years technologically to recover genuine values.

L. What might it mean to speak of a language that existed only through its syntax? Would that still be a language? Doesn't that run entirely counter to the human striving which consists precisely in deploying language for purposes of communication?

BARTHES. I agree with you. Formalization is something of a fashion. Much as I don't think structuralism is a fashion, I do believe that formalization, the desire to subsume the discourse of the human sciences in algorithms and mathematical formulae, is a very general temptation but a wrong-headed one. A language has to exist through its lexicon or, in other words, through a certain impurity, through the polysemy that every lexicon represents and, indeed, that's represented by the introduction of a lexicon into a syntax.

M. Might the possibility for fantasy in the field of mathematics explain something of the pupils' failure to understand it?

BARTHES. You think there is fantasizing in the field of maths?

M. No, but among young children in particular, the ideas of straight lines and planes are very realist in their reference. As soon as we leave this realism behind, we try to symbolize in maths.

BARTHES. This is an area of asemia. The imagination of forms and relationships is an imagination of a highly developed kind and is wholly unrelated to that kind of absence of resonance or symbolic incapacity of the psychosomatic individual, for example. I spoke with a mathematician recently and was struck by the metaphorical character of his speech. This wasn't about formulae on a blackboard, but he was talking and his talk produced some very, very fine metaphors. I said to myself that if Bachelard had been there, he would have found it very easy to analyse the mathematician's metaphors as a poetic instrument.

GB. I wouldn't like to sidetrack the conversation on to what are perhaps rather marginal subjects, but I'm troubled to hear you assigning mathematics to the domain of asemia. In maths, there are always two entities present: you speak about something in the language of a certain theory and the two theories generally stand in a very clearly defined relationship. The discussion might be about geometry, about transformations, and I say: 'Isometries are a group.' This means that I'm going to speak about geometry in the language of group theory. Are these two fields in a relationship of signifier to signified? You constantly have a concretization of certain theories in various fields (this too is part of mathematics). Are these theories polysemic or asemic? A single field can be the concretization of several theories, of several structures, each structure being a certain way to talk about things. Structures are entangled in mathematics in such a way that there's always signifier and signified. Only there is never oneness. Nor does a term—even a basic term—necessarily have one practical meaning. You never say, 'This is concrete'. You say that it's a realization or, if you prefer, a concretization of a particular structure. And the application of mathematics to physics doesn't change that pattern—only certain data are declared concretely significant, so there isn't entirely a state of asemia. Though perhaps it is a state of asemia with respect to other things. Internally, on the other hand, such work is rigorously monosemic—each word has only one meaning in a theory. Having said that, choosing a particular model, within the private recesses of one's mind, may indeed give rise to some wild intentions. This is perhaps what Monsieur Meyer was referring to.[2] One talks about a situation in a language one chooses as convenient.

BARTHES. This brings us back to a current problem in semantics, the problem of context. Mathematics establishes its validity by context. It determines fields within which the language is established through context. Context is, in fact, a notion that is not known at all yet in linguistics, as it is very difficult to study. But context seems to be what has to provide the dialectical transition, to some degree, between syntax and semantics. From what you say, the languages of mathematics would ultimately seem to be languages that are both relational and contextual, but not lexical. Are there really signifiers and signifieds?

GB. Insofar as you distinguish two structures . . .

BARTHES. It seems to me you're on the side here of all those who now think that it's all about signifiers, since your structures are signifiers. You do indeed set them alongside in a temporary relationship of signifier to signified, but there isn't one of them that's a signified *in its essence*. Semiology has changed a lot in the last five years. Five or six years ago, we were still working with signifiers on the

---

2 It seems reasonable to assume that Mr Meyer is the speaker referred to earlier as M. [Trans.]

one side and signifieds on the other. Now we find, in reality, that everything's a lot more slippery. And operational concepts such as context are becoming much more important—or the concept of homologies between structures.

J. In the audiovisual field, we're in the realm of polysemy and it would be nice to move from that polysemy, which admits of interpretation, to a hierarchical polysemy, in order subsequently to arrive, perhaps, at a monosemy. In the experiment being attempted here, can we find methods for working on images and sound that would lead from a polysemy that admits of interpretation to a hierarchical polysemy—that's to say, one that would deliver a primary meaning?

In this connection, just as we were talking a moment ago about how context could, ultimately, eliminate asemia, I believe context can also progressively eliminate polysemy. Insofar as we bring together several images, each of these images having a different meaning, the polysemic field of interpretation of the isolated image will thereby be reduced to that of the string of images, which is itself relatively less polysemic than before.

BARTHES. You can't treat the image we traditionally call an art image—let's say a picture, a painting— like a press photo or a photograph from *Paris-Match* magazine, because it seems that art achieves a certain aesthetic level precisely to the degree that we can't rank hierarchically the various meanings we find in it. In a picture by Poussin, you can find a number of possible readings, but it's only ever by making certain prior assumptions that you'll attribute a kind of priority to one reading over another. With images of the *Paris-Match* type or advertising images, by contrast, reading them is a much more political problem—it falls more easily within the scope of the teacher, because quite simply it's a matter there perhaps of teaching the child to sort out the two or three more or less latent, more or less hidden, more or less intentional messages. With images there are possibilities of mystification, so merely exercising a critical spirit is important.

One of the possible tasks of an education in images might be to unsettle the pupil a little, to cast doubt on this sense of certainty felt towards the 'real' of photography. It seems to me that an educational task with respect to photography might consist, initially, in de-realizing photography, in leading the child to dialecticize this sort of superego of the real involved in it.

x. Isn't the fact of confronting a pupil with the polysemy of a photograph in itself one of the aims you're proposing?

BARTHES. Yes. Ultimately, just as a large part of the task of the teaching of literature is to sharpen what we've called the critical faculty—by which we mean a way of seeing the meanings that are underneath, all the possible meanings and the hidden ones—we should also do that to some extent with images, though perhaps in a more confident spirit than we do with texts, because the interpretation of a text has always been very monosemic in our teaching system, at least over the last fifty years or so.

x. Couldn't this very research you've been talking about have consequences at the educational level that would precisely be about learning to see polysemy?

BARTHES. Exactly. The problem is to recognize it. In a world condemned to signs, I believe that the basic ethical problem is to recognize signs *where they are*. In other words, not to mistake signs for natural phenomena and to announce their presence instead of concealing them. What we call mass culture can only be judged very ambiguously, very dialectically. It's very complicated, but if it has a failing, it's a culture that conceals the sign, that works on values that are always presented as natural and conceal the arbitrary character of the sign systems. If we look at contrasting civilizations, such as Eastern ones, we see civilizations that have lived with sign systems that are entirely declared as such, entirely on display. The Oriental theatre is a theatre in which everything is coded and the codes are announced as such—as codes—whereas

Western theatre is a theatre that naturalizes and realizes. Whatever the particular school of theatre, it attempts to conceal the sign beneath an idea of naturalness, so to speak. This is an educational problem, of course, but it seems to me that if I were teaching a class, spontaneously this is more or less what I'd do.

G. To what extent is aesthetics involved in how an image signifies?

BARTHES. Where advertising is concerned, I believe that aesthetics always also operates as a reference to aesthetics. Aesthetic values are never innocent— they are values that signify themselves *as aesthetic values*. These aesthetic values are themselves caught up in a code, the code of aesthetics, which in advertising is rather elementary. My answer here merely shifts the question back a level, because we have to ask: Are there actually aesthetic values? And what are they?

Ideally, a good structural analysis ought to be able to account for aesthetics in structural terms.

MADAME P. Given that the cinema doesn't know the code of all social realities, it provides an interpretation and generally traduces the subject it's dealing with. Art films never express what they're trying to.

BARTHES. This very much connects with my reaction to cinema. Cinema gives me a major problem— I'd almost be inclined to say that nothing has happened since [Sergei] Eisenstein, in a sense. You get the impression that it's actually an art that doesn't yet have its culture. For that reason, it's very difficult to speak of cinema at the moment. I'm particularly struck by the fact that those we call the younger directors—making a cinema that may, incidentally, have values which are liberatory in character—are dominated by a kind of anti-intellectualism, which means that all sign-related problems are denied in the name of an 'objective reality'. There is, in fact, an interesting theory of the sign defined by André Breton.

This is the so-called *saccade* theory—there are signs everywhere, but you have to know how to recognize them, then how to cut them out from the real. This *saccade* that makes the sign visible also destroys it as reality. Modern art is always trying to prevent meaning from 'taking'...

Cahiers Média 1 (1970). Published by the Centre régional de documentation pédagogique, Bordeaux.

The Linguistics of Discourse

Oeuvres complètes, Volume 3, pp. 611–16

The following rather pithy text, which was published in Algirdas Julien Greimas, Roman Jakobson, Maria Renata Mayenowa, S. K. Šaumjan, Wilhelm Steinitz and S. Zoliewski (eds), *Sign, Language, Culture / Signe, langage, culture* (Janua Linguarum, series maior 1) (Paris: Mouton, 1970), pp. 580–84, reflects Barthes's oft-expressed concern during these years—that linguistic analysis should seek ways to find a junction with the 'extra-semiological disciplines such as history, psychology or aesthetics'.

1. The folk tale, the short story, the myth, poetry and style—in short, all those things that can conveniently, but not very rigorously, be termed literature—have already had a range of structural approaches applied to them, as well as giving rise to important studies that are currently under way. Because of their diverse origins (in ethnology, literary criticism, content analysis or linguistics), these analyses are often pitched at different levels: some propose to study functions or figures (the poetic function and metaphor and metonymy in the case of Jakobson), others distributional units ('the functions of the folk tale' in the case of Propp, connected speech for Harris).

Working solely from the standpoint of a classification of semiotics, we propose to unify these efforts, together with those to which the infinitely varied works of folklore, literature and a part of mass communications (the part involving written or spoken *parole*) will inevitably give rise, under a single semiotics, which we shall call, provisionally at least, the linguistics of discourse or translinguistics (the preferable term of meta-linguistics having already been claimed for a different purpose).

2. The principle of unification of the objects of translinguistics stems from the unity of their substance—in all cases, it is *parole* that is at issue, written or spoken. All translinguistic systems are therefore subject to the single constraint of articulated language—the linearity of the message. Successional signs predominate greatly over simultaneous signs. The effects of linearity on translinguistic systems haven't yet been studied very much; they are nonetheless crucial, since the linearity of signs, by imposing the fundamental irreversibility of the message on users, leads them to develop, in compensation, a whole set of reversibility operators, as we see in narrative and poetic languages. The unit of linguistic substance brings together certain systems, but it forces us also to divide certain 'genres'; a distinction will be made, for example, between the word-based narrative [*le récit-parole*] and the image-based narrative [*le récit-image*]. If these two modes of narrative have a—properly 'diegetic'—common structure, this can only be described a posteriori at a higher level, coextensive with the semiotics of pure time (irreversibility) and the semiotics of time/space (reversibility).

3. Translinguistic systems are built upon articulated language, the object of linguistics; they are not however coterminous with it. The object studied by linguistics is confined to a purpose of pure communication; the objects offered to translinguistics no doubt also have that purpose, since their substance is linguistic, but in them the function of communication is diversified and specialized in accordance with a number of secondary aims. It is commonly understood that a work [*oeuvre*] involves an object of communication, but also that that object is communicated for aesthetic or persuasive purposes, for purposes of entertainment or ritual, etc., and that these aims are not in any sense contingent but are codified by society. If we call the object of translinguistics *discourse* (making it homologous with the *text* on which linguistics works), we may give the following provisional definition of that discourse as *any finite range of* parole, *unified from the standpoint of content, emitted and structured for secondary purposes of communication, and culturalized by factors other than those of language.*

4. The territory of translinguistics (or territory of discourse) may thus be defined in terms of linguistics, since linguistics and translinguistics each have the same substance. Now we know that, for the moment at least, linguistics stops at the sentence. This is not the place to delve into the debate that has grown up around the concept of sentence (we would not be competent to do so); we shall confine ourselves to citing Émile Benveniste's clarification of the question, because he refers to the sentence as the upper *limit* of the linguistic object.[1] We shall sum up Benveniste's

---

1 'The Levels of Linguistic Analysis', *Problems in General Linguistics* (Oxford, OH: University of Miami Press, 1973), pp. 101–11.

thinking as follows: A sentence can be defined only by its constituents. It can be segmented but it cannot be integrated into anything. It is the last level of integration of linguistic signs; it contains signs but it isn't a sign. With sentences, then, we leave linguistics and enter upon a new area of description—namely, the description of discourse, of which the sentence may be a unit. The sentence is therefore a hinge between text and discourse; as Benveniste notes: '[I]t conveys both meaning and reference: meaning because it is informed by signification, and reference because it refers to a given situation.'[2] From a taxonomic point of view, the territory of translinguistics lies, then, *beyond the sentence*.

5. This territory is immense. It has already been explored. First, by Aristotle and his successors who attempted to divide (non-mimetic) discourse into units of increasing size, from the sentence to the major parts of the *dispositio*, by way of the 'period' and the 'passage' (*ekphrasis, descriptio*). Then, in overtly structural terms by our contemporaries: the Russian Formalist school, Jakobson, [Yuri] Scheglov and his Soviet colleagues, [Zellig S.] Harris, and [Nicolas] Ruwet, not forgetting the ethnologists, who have lent a crucial impetus to the structural analysis of myths (Propp and Lévi-Strauss).

2 Ibid., p. 110.

ROLAND BARTHES

From the epistemological point of view, that is to say, from a viewpoint coextensive with all this research, an important problem still has to be resolved—namely, the problem of the exhaustiveness of descriptions. For example, between Harris' 'connected speech' and Propp's 'functions', which are entirely detached from the verbal substance, it is clear that a narrative— a novel, for example—has in it an enormous quantity of messages which, extending beyond the sentence, are not covered by any kind of description. The sieve is, so to speak, too fine-meshed (catching only linguistic matter) or too coarse-meshed (catching units that might be extra-linguistic). A linguistics reduced to phonology and grammar would be similarly unsatisfactory.

Exhaustivity, not of *description* but of *descriptions*, is an essential demand of every science. What lies beyond the sentence will therefore have to be described exhaustively: on the one hand, it must be possible to situate any item of information provided by the letter of the corpus at a systematic level of description; on the other, these levels taken together must form an integrated continuum, with each unit of one level acquiring its meaning, as Benveniste's formulation has it, only by its insertion in units of the level immediately above, as is successively the case with the feature (merism), the phoneme and the word (we have seen that the sentence, linguistically speaking, integrates the word, but cannot itself be integrated into anything else). Translinguistics cannot, then, be constituted unless it establishes, for each of its objects, the levels of integration of discourse, from the sentence—the last level of linguistic integration and the first level of translinguistic integration—to the point where the discourse is articulated to social *praxis*.

6. The need for integrative description is not only epistemological but also operational, since it is on that description that the segmentation of discourse into units depends. Substitution, which is necessary for segmentation (at least we believe this to be so), can in fact only be carried out in the name of meaning. And meaning, according to Benveniste's formulation, to which we refer once again, depends on integrative relations formed between levels, not on distributional relations formed between elements of a single level. In other words, in order to commutate, we have to know on what basis we are commutating. For its part, linguistic commutation is carried out, if we may put it this way, on the basis of the 'raw' meaning that is necessary for pure communication, to the exclusion of any other function of the message. But beyond the sentence, in the world of discourse, meaning becomes inevitably referential; it is determined in relation to a situation, outside of which the new commutation cannot take effect. Paul Valéry pointed out that the phrase 'open the door' had no meaning out in the desert, but that it reacquired a meaning if the desert was metaphorical, etc. Taken in the raw state, the utterance does indeed have a meaning, but that meaning is merely linguistic. To move into the translinguistic sphere is precisely to give the utterance a supplementary meaning. Placed, for example, in a narrative situation, the utterance will be available for a new commutation that will determine whether or not it is necessary for the succession of functions and whether, as a consequence, it can be defined as a sign segment. In other words, so long as the utterance isn't situated, it remains, from the standpoint of discourse, a mere non-signifying, propositional function. To transform that function into a proposition, it has to be subjected to a new pertinence, which is that of its situation. We know all this already. We are henceforth proposing, however, to give situations of discourse full structural value, since, on the one hand, they determine a certain hierarchy of integrative levels and, on the other, they enable the new translinguistic commutation to take place.

7. Initial situations (for example, the narrative situation) correspond directly to the communication that unites the sender of the discourse (Narrator) to the receiver (Narratee)—this is not the case for the subsequent levels (for example, characters or functions) which are entirely subject to the referential function (the content of the story). Therefore, the narrative situation, for example, constitutes a level of autonomous description; all the more so as it has signifiers of its own available to it. Poetic communication has its own which have been strictly codified over a long period, as has narrative (for example, the simple past in French). It is possible that the systematic analysis of situations of discourse will lead us to modify the traditional distinction between genres; it is possible also that it will confirm it. This matters little; what is important is to have a solid first level which makes it possible subsequently to integrate the other levels in the hierarchical series. The number of these levels certainly varies, depending on the starting level (or 'finishing' level, depending on whether we come at discourse from its minimal units or its major functions); in lyric poetry, it is probably the case that the lower units—the distributional development of a single metaphor—are directly articulated to the lyric situation; by contrast, in narrative, the minimal units—indices or terms of functions—pass through several integrating relays (function, actant) before connecting with the properly narrative level. The number and organization of the integratory levels may therefore be a criterion for the classification of discourses. It is the same with distributional relations, once the levels of integration have been established. Narrative, for example, certainly seems to be characterized by what, at the linguistic level, [Charles] Bally called *dystaxia* or a break in the forward-moving linearity of the spoken sequence—in narrative, the terms of a single function may be either distended and separated by very long infixes or inserts (*suspense*) or even reversed and anticipated (*feedback*), unlike intellectual discourse which operates on a progressive model.

8. To sum up this brief contribution, I shall recall what seem to me to be the two principles necessary for establishing a semiotics of discourse. The first of these specifies the way in which translinguistics takes over where linguistics leaves off. Linguistics stops at the sentence, because the sentence is something purely predicative and, apart from 'meaning', it invariably involves a reference, which linguistics has always refused to code, even though the new demands of semantics, of automatic translation and of the very concept of grammaticality are increasingly bringing further to the fore the notion of *context* or *situation*. It is, all in all, this concept that is the sphere of translinguistics; the essential task of that discipline is to code reference. We may say that rhetoric, the ancestor of translinguistics, also had as its object for centuries to establish a code of speaking (admittedly, a normative one), and that, in order to establish that code, it too began by carefully distinguishing between certain situations of discourse (mimetic, deliberative, judicial, epidictic). In a word, the referential is extra-linguistic and intra-semiological.

The second principle brings us back to linguistics. The system of discourse more or less homographically reproduces the system of the sentence with its two coordinates: on the one hand, substitution, segmentation and distributional relations between segments of the same level and, on the other, integration of the units of each level into a higher-level unit that lends it meaning. We believe it is crucial to consider discourse not only as a distributional ensemble (as is done, for example, by Propp, since his functions all unfold on a single level) but also as an integrated ensemble. The principle of integration has a twofold impact: first, of course, it has a structural impact, since, theoretically, it allows meaning to be described and, operationally, it enables discourse to be segmented; second, it has a general impact, since it enables us to attribute a descriptive status to the *limit* of the system by pointing, *in semiological terms* (this is the important aspect), to the moment when the system is articulated to social and historical praxis. A semiotics that respects the principle of integration has every chance of cooperating effectively with extra-semiological disciplines such as history, psychology or aesthetics.

From A. J. Greimas et al. (eds), *Sign, Language, Culture / Signe, langage, culture* (Paris: Mouton, 1970), pp. 580–4.

On Theory

The following interview was given to the Zurich-based avant-garde magazine *VH 101*, edited by the Viennese-born art critic Otto Hahn and Françoise Esselier, and published in its second issue in August 1970. Other contributors included writers Alain Robbe-Grillet and Philippe Sollers, academics Pierre Bourdieu, Lucien Goldmann, Claude Lévi-Strauss, Jean-François Lyotard, André Martinet, J.-B. Pontalis, Olivier Revault d'Allonnes and Bernard Teyssèdre, architect Yona Friedman and artist Victor Vasarely. *VH 101* did not survive beyond its ninth issue, dated Winter 1972.

The study of Balzac's *Sarrasine* to which Barthes refers is his celebrated *S/Z* (Paris: Éditions du Seuil, 1970), the English translation of which was published by Hill and Wang of New York in 1974.

Oeuvres complètes, Volume 3, pp. 689–96

VH 101. Can structural analysis be built up into a theory or is it just a set of systems or mechanisms that are applied as the text seems to require?

ROLAND BARTHES. Your question covers everything I have to say about theory. We need to begin from a more precise starting point.

VH 101. Is the analysis carried out through a set of systems that aren't formed into a theory, or does a general theory emerge from the analysis?

BARTHES. I'd like to say first that theory isn't to be taken to mean abstraction; hence it isn't opposed to the concrete. I don't think we can understand the word as they did in the nineteenth century, as a kind of general representation of concepts. This is the meaning you still find in dictionaries like [André] Lalande's *Dictionnaire philosophique*. Moreover, as is to be expected of an age in which a sort of empirical, scientistic rationalism predominated, the word 'theory' had a generally rather pejorative sense. It was invariably contrasted, not with practice in the Marxist sense of the term but with experience, with the test of fact, in keeping with the model—or, at any rate, under the aegis—of the superego of the experimental sciences. As I see it, then, theory isn't an abstraction and isn't the opposite of the concrete.

As a result, I could very well imagine analysing a text and doing so with an avowedly theoretical intent. Indeed, I've imagined such an analysis and I've tried to carry it out. My commentary on Balzac's *Sarrasine* (1830) was both an analysis of the text and, as I see it, a theory of the text—of the classical text, the readable text. The second thing is that, where the mode of exposition is concerned, the word theory commonly connotes a sustained discourse, a sustained presentation on the classical philosophical model, an exposition in the style of the academic essay with all the constraints of argument and vocabulary which that implies. Against this, I could very well imagine—and would even like to see—discourses taking on a degree of discontinuity, showing a degree of fragmentariness in their exposition, not unlike speech acts of an aphoristic or poetic type, and such discourses being able to constitute a fundamentally theoretical discourse. Moreover, I think we're seeing tentative steps towards such a theoretical discourse, which might be said to break with the rhetorical habits of scholarship, in books like Lévi-Strauss' *Mythologiques* (1964), for example. I also believe that Jacques Lacan's style of utterance is to be understood as an attempt to break with the continuous thread of discourse, with the sequential nature of theoretical writing in general. These are the first two obstacles I'd like to clear out of the way—theory isn't to be confounded with abstraction or with oratory.

Now, as for defining what theory is, someone very close to my position (or someone whose position I'm very close to), Julia Kristeva, has done this in very sustained fashion in her book *Semeiotike* (1969) which is precisely a work of theory. Let me add the following. As I've said, we can't keep to the nineteenth-century definition. The etymology of the word pointed towards an *action* of observing or contemplating, a meditation or speculation. I found somewhere the following definition: 'That which is the object of a disinterested knowledge, irrespective of its applications.' Ultimately, the theoretical was the opposite of the applied. I think this is an inadequate definition today, at least with regard to the field of my thinking, which is that of semiotics or, more particularly, literary and textual semiotics, since theory here is essentially a scientific discourse that isn't an abstract, generalizing or foundational discourse but additionally— and this is its distinctive feature—a discourse that reflects on itself. A language that reflects back on itself.

VH 101. That seeks out its own laws?

BARTHES. Yes . . . that observes itself in a kind of permanent self-criticism. And it's probably pursuing itself in order to destroy itself. But it doesn't destroy itself immediately, and that kind of stay of execution produces theory.

VH 101. So theory has periodically to be re-cast?

BARTHES. Absolutely. Theory is, ultimately, a complete discourse—that is to say, a reflexive one—but it's permanently on borrowed time. And the reflexivity obviously mustn't be conceived as something circular and closed . . . . It isn't about locking up a truth in a theory. But discourse, while thinking itself as signifier and criticizing itself as discourse, must escape the two constraints I mentioned at the beginning—namely, abstraction and the discursive thread or continuity. I wonder whether, in the end, we might not regard theory and *écriture* as one and the same. *Écriture*, in the current sense we can give to that word, is a theory. It has a theoretical dimension and no theory must reject *écriture*; in other words, it must not deploy itself solely within pure *écrivance*—that is to say, a purely instrumental view of the language it uses.

VH 101. Robbe-Grillet says that if theory is valid, there's no need for literary works [*oeuvres*] any more.

BARTHES. In a sense that's true. In any event, it can come about that there's no distinction between literary works and theory any more. I take the view, for example, that Kristeva's book on semiotics is a 'work' like the works Robbe-Grillet produces or might have produced.

VH 101. In an interview published recently in *Le Nouvel Observateur*, Sartre said: 'I'd like my *Flaubert* to be read the way you read a novel, because I put certain objective facts into it, but there are lots of things I reconstituted or invented . . .'

BARTHES. I can very well understand this desire, insofar as I don't believe at all in the separation of genres. I think that what's still called the discourse of the essay or of criticism is going to be reworked, is going to undergo a profound subversion in a way that's currently being worked out, while, broadly speaking, one can't write novels any more. This is being worked out in the area of text, not in the area of the novel or poetry. The notion of text is inevitably going to come to encompass the essay and criticism—in short, what was until now termed intellectual or even scientific discourse. At that point, there will be texts in the current, strong sense of the word, and these will, as texts, be theoretical—they'll have a theoretical dimension and impact.

VH 101. Isn't theory a projection of the problems human beings set themselves? In every age, texts have been taken up again and given an up-to-date interpretation. So works are constantly being reinterpreted, so to speak. Is this a society or the representatives of a society projecting themselves anew into that work? Or is there indeed such a thing as a meaning in itself, defined theoretically?

BARTHES. That wouldn't prevent the work [*l'oeuvre*] from being defined theoretically. Theory, as I've attempted to come at it, doesn't set out truths or values in themselves but in relation to historical development. And here I'll say that the theoretical exigency that's currently emerging for some of us is bound up with a definite historical and political situation. We might very well imagine—and I think we have to—that a society of a socialist type, in the precise sense this term has in Marxism—a society that isn't yet communist but is no longer capitalist, as we might imagine the new China to be—no longer has to produce theory in the Western sense of the word. I think Mao said some quite precise things about this. In the experience of current China, he doesn't want theory to be separated from practice and he doesn't want there to be specialists in theory or, in other words, intellectuals, this point being related to the socialist contention that manual and intellectual labour are not to be separated. In the new China, it's the people in itself that is, as it were, at every moment, its own theorist. But I don't believe the analysis of Western Maoists to be correct when they seek to apply this conception to the Western situation. In a society of a capitalist type like ours, I believe theory is precisely the type of progressive discourse that's made both possible and necessary by *this* society, which is transitory and pre-socialist in character. In other words, there can be said to be a historical correspondence between our society and theoretical activity insofar as it's the progressive activity that can be tolerated by this society as its own seed of destruction—we *must*, therefore, perform this theoretical activity.

VH 101. You seem to be saying that in a society without need, theory is superfluous since human beings will no longer be trying to get out of one situation and into another—there will be a complete acceptance of the situation.

BARTHES. That's not what I mean. Human beings will no longer need a discourse of a reflexive or intellectual type. Theory will be entirely politicized. It will be *in* the revolution itself and hence, at that point, there'll no longer be any grounds for setting theory against practice. Practice will be entirely theoretical and vice versa. And I think it's more or less already like that in China.

VH 101. Perhaps I'm extrapolating your thinking, but you seem to be saying that theory is produced by the anxiety of human beings who are in search of themselves among significations.

BARTHES. Not at all. I'm not giving a neurotic definition of theory. I conceive these matters in terms of semiotics rather than in terms of 'neurotics'. Let me say that theory is what enables work and research to be taken forward without our being locked into a signified of the type we now term 'transcendental', whether that signified be God or *ratio*—reason—or science. Theory, precisely if we conceive it as a permanent self-criticism, is constantly dissolving the signified which is ever-ready to become reified under the cover of science. It's for this reason, as I said a little while ago, that theory is articulated to writing as the realm of the signifier.

VH 101. You say in *S/Z* that there's a science of the text, assuming that there can be a scientific knowledge about the text . . .

BARTHES. We have to be clear what's meant by 'scientific'. I don't understand science in the sense of a scientistic scientificity which shelters behind a kind of knowledge that could be said to have, as it were, an absolute subject. I draw on the analyses of science made by Lacan, Althusser and Kristeva. There's a science of the text because the text isn't grasped by a subjectivity of an impressionistic type, but through a science of the real of a Marxist type and a science of the subject of a Freudian type. It's insofar as these things apply that there's a science of the text.

VH 101. There's a phrase I didn't understand. You speak of 'a liberatory theory of the signifier'.[1]

---

1 The phrase comes from the back cover of the French edition of *S/Z*. [Trans.]

Should we understand this as a 'liberatory theory on the part of the signifier' or 'a theory liberating the signifier'?

BARTHES. I use the expression in both senses: recourse to the signifier liberates, and it's also a question of liberating the signifier from the signified. I mean that all around us the signified is generally coming to be put in the dock, so to speak. This was set in train by Lévi-Strauss' thinking in the first instance, whatever he may think of it now . . .

VH 101. Speaking of Lévi-Strauss, he claims not to model his activity on a theory . . .

BARTHES. No doubt in the name of a certain empirical rationalism . . . . However that may be, this challenge to the signified is currently being mounted by people like Lacan, Derrida and Kristeva. In the work they're doing, the aim is to drive out the signified as representative of monology, theology, scientism, the origin, filiation, determination, etc.—everything that fails to take account of multiplicity, the plurality of the world and its organization along the lines of a fluctuating hierarchy.

VH 101. Why perform analysis on works, on texts, and not on language itself? Why this turn towards works of art which ultimately represent only a very limited part of society?

BARTHES. Analysing language itself isn't to be ruled out, but where could we lay hands on this 'language itself'? It's not entirely clear. If it's in spoken language, then at that point we'd be abolishing the distinction between the spoken word and writing. What's precious in works of a classical type is that, though they belong to a period that pre-dates modernity, they're nonetheless written. There is writing—*écriture*—that goes into those works. This is a very important fact when it comes to refining the analysis of the signifier and limiting the damage that would be done by the analysis of an object like spoken language and *parole*, which is, after all, very much bogged down in expressivity. Whereas writing, even classical writing, has put some distance between itself and the spoken word—that is why it is precious for these first analyses. Now if, within these written works, I've settled on a *single* work, this is because works in that form of literature are 'closed'. They're con- structed as narratives that have an ending.

VH 101. There's already a system there? . . .

BARTHES. It's the system of the readable. In this case the work is closed—this is the reason for studying *one* work. But if you want to analyse genuinely plural texts like those of Lautréamont, as I've already done, the idea of closure no longer applies at all and you have to move between text and intertext. There, the text is caught up in an infinite interplay, which clearly isn't the case with Balzac.

VH 101. You say, too, that the *Tel Quel* group is producing one of the only bodies of theoretical work at the moment. What do you mean by that?

BARTHES. I believe they are. They are producing genuinely theoretical work, insofar as they have themselves helped to specify what the requirements of theory are. And it's those requirements I'm concerned with, in the sense that I've tried to give to the word.

VH 101. Is it possible in present-day society, subject as it is to the needs we encounter daily in capitalist society, to produce a purified theory in the way Sollers does, to take a stance external to all ideology, a liberatory stance? . . . We're back with [Francis] Ponge here and his creation of a post-revolutionary body of work . . .

BARTHES. It's inevitable. We're at that moment in a history, in our history, which requires that all our forces are invested in a negativity. Hence theory's superiority over literary works. We might very well imagine a period—our own, for example—in which theory is produced and not works. And, indeed, there are very few works at the moment—I'm talking here about what's commonly termed literature. On the other hand, there's undeniable theoretical activity. I believe this is the mark of our decade. I don't know what will happen after . . .

VH 101. How has a society of a certain type come to want to pose anti-historical problems, problems outside history, problems which leave history behind altogether?

BARTHES. Oh no, we're not outside history. We have to be more specific about this. What's been going on for the last five years—and it was absolutely *necessary*, it was really a necessary clear-out because we were suffocating, or, at any rate, I'm from a generation that was suffocating—has been an attempt to theorize a historical pluralism. Up to that point we had a purely linear, purely deterministic history, a history that was monist, so to speak, and structuralism helped us to acquire this awareness of a historical pluralism. We're not trying to leave history behind but, rather, to complicate it. What's going on is, as the scientists say, a complexification—and this is more or less a good thing. It's in this sense that Sollers spoke at one point of a 'monumental history'—a historical heritage that doesn't have the same wavelength, so to speak, as other histories that are internal to it. I'd say that what seems quite revolutionary in theory—at any rate, what's often contested and encounters resistance—has already been postulated in the historical sciences by historians like [Lucien] Febvre or [Fernand] Braudel—the coexistence of structures of differing wavelengths.

VH 101. To come back to yourself, you're much less interested in meaning itself than in the mechanism of meaning?

BARTHES. As I see it, that's quite a normal development. At the time of *Mythologies* I saw things in what was clearly a simpler way. On the one hand there were languages, as we might put it—broadly speaking, signifiers—and, on the other, there was a socio-historical signified which was, broadly speaking, the mental structure of the French petty bourgeoisie, expressed mainly in mass culture. This was a rather archaeological view of the sign, with its two parts, the signifier and the signified. What I've now learnt from others—it's the others around me who've taught me this—is that it's actually necessary to go further and cast doubt not just on a particular type of signified but on the sign itself, the signifying relation itself. One might then give the impression of freeing oneself from contingent history, of floating outside of time, but in fact the battle to fissure the Western symbolic has already begun, here and now. I think we started it quite a few years ago. This is a great adventure that's beginning. Perhaps it'll be halted, because barbarism is always a possibility, but all in all, so long as it's possible, we're fighting this battle.

VH 101 (Summer 1970)

A Very Fine Gift

This brief article in *Le Monde* (16 October 1971) was a tribute, on his seventy-fifth birthday, to the Russo-American scholar Roman Jakobson, one of the pioneers of structural linguistics, particularly in its applications to literary theory. Barthes probably first read Jakobson on the recommendation of Greimas, shortly after Greimas had also introduced him to the work of Saussure.

The quotation from Jakobson withwhich the article ends is from 'Linguistics and Poetics', *Language in Literature* (Cambridge, MA: The Belknap Press of Harvard University Press, 1987), p. 94.

Oeuvres complètes, Volume 3, pp. 885–6

Jakobson made literature a very fine gift—he gave it linguistics. Admittedly, Literature didn't need Roman Jakobson to tell it it was Language—the whole of classical Rhetoric, up to the work of Paul Valéry, attests to the fact; but as soon as a science of language came to be pursued (initially in the form of a historical and comparative linguistics of languages), it strangely lost interest in meaning-effects, itself succumbing, in that positivistic century—the nineteenth—to the taboo of separate spheres or provinces, with Science, Reason and Fact on the one side and Art, Sensibility and Impressions on the other. From his youth, Jakobson was involved in rectifying this situation—because this linguist was always intent on remaining a great lover of poetry, painting and cinema; and because, within his scientific research, he didn't censure his pleasures as a cultivated individual, he was aware that the true scientific achievement of modernity lay in determining not facts but relations. At the origins of the generalized linguistics he mapped out, there was a decisive act of opening up classifications, castes and disciplines—with his work, these words lost their separatist, penal, racist overtones; there are no longer any proprietors (of Literature or Linguistics) and the watchdogs have been sent back to their enclosures.

Jakobson bestowed three things on Literature. First, he created a special department within Linguistics—namely, Poetics. He didn't define this sector (and this is what is new in his work, his historic contribution) by starting out from Literature (as though Poetics always depended on 'the poetic' or on 'poetry'), but on the basis of the analysis of language functions: every speech-act that stresses the form of the message is poetic; as a result, he was able, *on the basis of a linguistic position*, to get back to the vital (and often most emancipated) forms of Literature—the entitlement to ambiguity of meaning, the system of substitutions, the code of figures (metaphor and metonymy).

Second, he called even more strongly than Saussure for a pansemiotics, a generalized (and not just a general) science of signs. Here again, however, his position is doubly avant-garde since, on the one hand, he retains a pre-eminent place in that science for articulated language (he well knows that language is *everywhere* and not just *alongside*), and, on the other, he immediately appends the fields of Art and Literature to semiotics, thus assuming from the outset that semiology is the science of signification and not of mere communication (in this way, he removes from linguistics any risk of a technocratic purpose or usage).

Lastly, his linguistics itself admirably lays the ground for the way we are able to conceive of the

Text today—namely, that the meaning of a sign is in fact simply its translation into another sign, which is to define meaning not as an ultimate signified but as *another* signifying level; namely, too, that the most ordinary language involves a significant number of meta-linguistic utterances, attesting to the need for human beings to think their language at the very same time as they speak it. This is a crucial activity which Literature merely raises to the highest degree of incandescence.

The very style of his thought, a brilliant, generous, ironic, expansive, cosmopolitan, nimble style, which we might also describe as *fiendishly intelligent*, predisposed Jakobson to this historical function of opening up, of abolishing disciplinary ownership. Another style is no doubt possible, based on both a more historical culture and a more philosophical conception of the speaking subject—I am thinking here of the unforget-table (and yet, as it seems to me, somewhat forgotten) writings of Benveniste, which should never be left out (Jakobson would agree here) of any *homage* to the decisive role of linguistics in the birth of that *other thing* that is at work in our century. Through all the novel and irreversible propositions that his fifty-year-long work consists in, Jakobson is, for his part, the his-torical actor who, by a deployment of intelligence, has consigned definitively *to the past* a number of very respectable things we held dear—he turns prejudice into anachronism. All his efforts remind us that 'All of us . . . definitely realize that a linguist deaf to the poetic function of language and a literary scholar indifferent to linguistic problems and unconversant with linguistic methods are equally flagrant anachronisms.'

Le Monde (16 October 1971)

Letter to Jean Ristat

Oeuvres complètes, Volume 4, p. 125

The following piece was published on 29 March 1972 in *Les Lettres françaises*, at that time a literary magazine financially supported by the French Communist Party, with Louis Aragon its editor-in-chief and Jean Ristat as one of his assistants. It ceased publication later that year as a result of financial difficulties resulting largely from the refusal of the Soviet authorities to continue to support it after it had criticized the invasion of Czechoslovakia in 1968. It has since been revived as a Saturday supplement to the Communist newspaper *L'Humanité* with Ristat as editor (as of 2015).

Barthes's letter came at a moment of great tension within French intellectual politics, shortly after the *Tel Quel* group had split with the French Communist Party, denouncing its revisionism and professing support for Maoist China and the Cultural Revolution. In this heated atmosphere, Jacques Derrida had agreed to a request from editor Antoine Casanova to grant an interview to the Communist Party journal *La Nouvelle Critique*. This apparently put him beyond the pale so far as certain members of *Tel Quel* were concerned, and the break that ensued was rather dramatic (Derrida and Philippe Sollers of *Tel Quel* had been close friends since 1964). In the circumstances, Ristat's decision to devote a special issue of *Les Lettres françaises* to Derrida, his former teacher and a friend of long standing, could easily be construed as an attempt to gather Derrida into the Communist camp.

The fact that, in the letter, Barthes declines Ristat's invitation to make a fuller contribution to the publication can be seen as a 'diplomatic' manoeuvre. Derrida's biographer writes: 'The lack of time was probably not the only reason for [excusing himsef]. Barthes was very close to Sollers and in a very delicate situation at this time when everyone was being forced to take sides.'[1] However, the letter *was* published in the review, alongside contributions from such as Jean Genet, Roger Laporte, Claude Ollier and Catherine Clément, and it seems that Derrida was genuinely touched by Barthes's tribute and wrote on 30 March to thank his 'dear friend' for his kind remarks.

1 Benoît Peeters, *Derrida: A Biography* (Cambridge: Polity, 2013), p. 235.

Paris, 21 March 1972

My dear Ristat,

For material reasons of time and tiredness, I cannot participate fully in the pages *Lettres françaises* is intending to devote to the work of Derrida. I am sorry that this is the case.

I belong to a different generation from Derrida—and probably from his readers. I therefore encountered his writings in midlife, as my work was developing. I had already clearly formed the semiological project and part of it was fulfilled, but there was a danger of its remaining confined in—and magically constrained by—the phantasm of scientificity. Derrida was among those who helped me to understand what the (philosophical, ideological) stakes of my own work were. He disrupted the balance of the structure and opened up the sign. He is, for us, *the person who unhooked the end of the chain*. His literary interventions (on [Antonin]

Artaud, Mallarmé and Bataille) were decisive, by which I mean that they were irreversible. We are indebted to him for new words, active words (in this regard his writing is something violent, poetic), and for a kind of unremitting erosion of our sense of intellectual comfort (that state in which we derive solace from our own thinking). Lastly, there is in his work something unsaid, which is fascinating—his solitude comes from what he has yet to say.

These are the ideas I would like to have put into proper shape (instead of merely articulating them). Once again, I'm sorry that I'm not able to do so at the moment.

Yours in friendship.

Les lettres francaises (29 March 1972)
special issue on Jacques Derrida.

For a Theory
of Reading

*Oeuvres
complètes,*
Volume 4,
pp. 171–3

This is another text that was published by a Centre régional de documentation pédagogique—in this case that of Orléans-Tours, which covers France's Centre region. France has a network of these CRDPs, in most cases one in each of the administrative regions of its education system (known as *academies*). Broadly speaking, it is the function of these centres to provide teachers with materials and information, a role which includes, as in this case, the dissemination of work originating in universities and other institutions of higher learning to classroom teachers in the wider national education system, to which end they organize talks and conferences. This text dates from a conference held at Tours, one of the two university towns in the region, on 23 November 1972.

At this point in his career, Barthes was not only teaching at the École pratique des hautes études but was also a visiting professor at the University of Geneva (invited there by Jean Starobinski and Jean Rousset), a contributor to Jean Bollack's seminar at Lille and a participant in Jean-Luc Nancy and Philippe Lacoue-Labarthe's research group at Strasbourg.

For twenty years or so now there has existed a *theory of writing*, elaborated in various ways. The aim of that theory has been to substitute for the old 'work–author' pairing, which absorbed all the energy of literary criticism and scholarship for a century, a new 'writing–reading' pairing. The new theory therefore postulates a theory of reading, but it must be admitted that this second theory is much less developed than the first. It is time now to work on it, first because there has never before been a theory of reading—the only idea we have had of the 'reader' so far has been vaguely projective: the reader 'is said to project himself' into the writer's work (as in Baudelaire's 'Hypocrite lecteur, mon semblable, mon frère' or Bachelard's conception of the reader as the ghost of the writer)—second, because it is possible today to have some new sciences converge on this problem of reading—sociology, semiology, psychoanalysis and even history—and, lastly, because there is currently, if not a crisis then at least a mutation in the technical and social conditions of reading.

A theory will soon be necessary then. 'Theory' here does not necessarily mean 'philosophical dissertation' or 'abstract system'. 'Theory' means description; it means a form of production that draws on diverse sciences and generates a responsible discourse that examines the problem in its infinite reach and freely opens itself to criticism as a discourse of scientificity.

*

There is much talk today of *interdisciplinarity*—it is more or less the pet theme of the new university system. But interdisciplinarity cannot merely consist in juxtaposing different disciplines: it consists—or, rather, will consist—in dialectically destroying each established discipline in favour of a brand new one. If I speak of interdisciplinarity here, that is because reading genuinely is an interdisciplinary problem if ever there was one: What goes on in the total act of reading? Where does reading begin? How far does it extend? Can we assign a structure or boundaries to this production? We shall have to draw on many disciplines to answer these questions. Reading is an *overdetermined* phenomenon, involving different levels of description. *Reading is what does not stop.*

The following—to offer a crude and provisional approximation—are the main levels of the act of reading and the main sciences that can be deployed in pinpointing and describing these levels:

1. *The Perceptual Level.* Perception of visual entities, problems of learning, rapid reading, internalized

reading: physiology, experimental psychology and the physio-psychology of reading (USA).

2. *The Denotative Level.* Comprehension of messages, the linguistics of communication.

3. *The Associative (Connotative) Level.* Development of symbolic associations of secondary meanings, of interpretations: the linguistics of signification, psychoanalysis, semiology.

4. *Intertextual Level.* Pressure of the stereotypes and/or earlier texts of the culture: semanalysis, socio-semiology of social codes.

To these levels we should also perhaps add two integrators on a permanent basis: the social code (levels of culture, class situation, ideological pressures); and desire, fantasy (levels and types of neuroses).

*

I should like to say, in conclusion, that a scientific description, even of a plural nature, will not cover the entirety of the phenomenon of reading. Reading, as we know, is a social object/issue; it is prey to instances of power and morality. This means that a theory of reading will have to accept being evaluative and being grounded in value. And, indeed, we have already been so in speaking of 'good' and 'bad' readings; the same is the case when we celebrate reading for its civilizing power. For my part, I shall formulate the ethical question in the following way: there are *dead* readings (subject to stereotypes, mental repetitions and sloganizing) and there are *living* readings (producing an inner text, homogeneous with a virtual writing on the part of the reader). Now, this living reading, during which the subject believes what he reads emotionally while also realizing its unreality, is a split reading. As I see it, it always involves the splitting of the subject Freud spoke of. It is based on a quite different logic from that of the *cogito*. And if we remember that, as Freud saw it, the splitting of the self is bound up with the various forms of perversion, we shall have to accept the idea that 'living reading' is a perverse activity and reading is always immoral.

Lecture et pédagogie. Actes du colloque tenu à Tours le 23 novembre 1972 (Orléans: CRDP, 1972)

Supplement

The first issue of *art press* magazine was dated December 1972–January 1973. As its joint founder and first editor Catherine Millet observed, it would not be what it is today if its history wasn't initially intertwined with that of *Tel Quel* and, in particular, if it hadn't been supported by leading figures from that journal, such as Philippe Sollers, Julia Kristeva and Marcelin Pleynet.

Oeuvres complètes, Volume 4, pp. 334–7

This short text, which Barthes contributed to *art press* 4 (May–June 1973), was conceived as a supplement to *Le Plaisir du texte*, which had appeared in January 1973 (Paris: Éditions du Seuil) and was subsequently published in English as *The Pleasure of the Text* (Richard Miller trans., with a Note on the Text by Richard Howard; New York: Hill and Wang, 1975).

Le Plaisir du texte is organized loosely and playfully around a series of key words in alphabetical order and the *Supplement* follow a similar pattern.

Dérive: Drift. Drifting is the active pursuit of a dis-
sociation. What is to be dissociated is the aggres-
sive consistency of languages [*langages*]. Hence
drifting is a practice of in-consistency. It isn't a
question of escaping from the war of languages
(even if you wanted to, you couldn't), but simply
this: aiming for an *elsewhere* that is *inside* (this is
precisely the image of the floating straw), thwar-
ting, by a thousand practices of writing, the power
grabs, the publicity offensives, the pledges—all
that will-to-possess [*vouloir-saisir*] that lurks in
the very *organization* of language.

Fiction: Fiction. As soon as a practice is taken in hand
by a discourse, a Fiction is produced. Our civilization experiences this slippage as inescapable—the
Book is inevitable. Where, then, are there practices
without books? Very far away, in Zen Buddhism,
for example. It is noteworthy that Zen rejects
the Book but not writing. Writing—going here by
the name of calligraphy— is something dissemi-
nated by Zen, but it disseminates it without textbooks, treatises or books. The pupil has simply to
watch the master and the—wordless—master isn't

caught in the toils of any kind of mastery: he doesn't 'transmit' knowledge, he doesn't collaborate in Fiction.

Jouissance: Bliss.[1] The very way reading is constituted makes it clandestine (the enigma of public libraries is that they are collections of clandestinity). One always reads furtively—it takes darkness for the 'decomposition of the subject's sensations' to take place, the profound surprise, the quickened beating of the heart that betokens bliss or fear.

Perpétuel: Perpetual. If the book is not conceived as arguing for an idea or giving an account of a destiny, if it refuses to afford itself depth and anchorage outside the signifier, it can only be perpetual, with no full stop to the text, no last word. And what is infinite in that book isn't only that its end doesn't come, but that at every point it is possible

---

1 The term 'bliss' has been much criticized as a translation of 'jouissance'. It is, however, the term that was used in the English translation of *Le Plaisir du texte* and it would seem unduly confusing to the general reader to change this particular horse in mid-stream. The critics have argued that 'bliss' has too much of an air of serenity about it (the phrase 'marital bliss' is often quoted as an example), but this, it seems to me, neglects the long-standing tradition of its use in theological texts to denote a state of barely expressible ecstasy. [Trans.]

to supplement it—something new can always grow later on in the interstices of its fabric, the interstices of the text. The book is holed—and that is where its productivity lies: I shall perhaps work on this slim volume my whole life long, supplementing it from within. This practice (which makes fragmentary writing obligatory) may possibly disconcert, for the perpetual book seems like a book *without a project* (without argument, without a summary, without will-to-possess)—it isn't going somewhere, it is just going; and it just keeps on going. The perpetual book isn't an eternal book.

Plaisir/Jouissance: Pleasure/Bliss. In *The Pleasure of the Text*, the opposition between pleasure and bliss is something of a trap. There's a kind of didactic gimmick on offer. A superficial material is being offered up, in a friendly way, to be summarized and reported. *Come on now*, give me your reading, bring it to me. Or, to put it a better way, the opposition becomes a false one only if you call on it to perform, if you ask it to provide a discriminative power, a criterion of judgement. It is true only within certain limits and these are not, in any sense, referential but discursive. The opposition exists only through its gradual elimination—through what it enables you to say and what remains once you have forgotten it. Don't ask this bone to contain any marrow whatever; don't call on it in relation to particular works or to history. It is a de-situated opposition, a discursive shifter.

Politique: Politics. What are we looking for? A new relationship between discourse and politics (this is called *écriture*). In the stereotypes of political language, we sensed the traces of a repetition or, in other words, of a failure. We would like a 'successful' language and we gradually discover, with astonishment, fear and outrage, that the language of the political sphere isn't necessarily political language. This is a gap neither of whose edges can be eliminated; duality is opened up here and heterology is at work. The political moulds a subject suffering total linguistic disorganization. But it is precisely that disorganization which is the work, which is the productivity and the 'remainder'—not the arrogances of political language, which for their part are merely dross. To get at the political, I have to use a roundabout language, to renounce straightforwardness—that is to say, the fictive solidarity of language.

This disorganization can have no other name than fear. Fear arises from the fact that *no one knows in your stead*—where beliefs end, writing [*écriture*] begins, which is the articulation (not the conjoining) of the political and bliss.

Productivité: Productivity. Once the book has appeared, the best readers' interventions (by definition, none of these is valueless since they contribute to the proliferation of the text) are those which are going to seek out (as good researchers might) *the clandestine points of productivity* in the reactive text. The finished (this simply means published) book inevitably includes the plan of an infinite work [*travail*]. In a book there are programmatic nodes which refer on to a work *yet to be done*. In *The Pleasure of the Text*, such nodes are no doubt: celebration as outbidding (with regard to Severo Sarduy), the differential rhythms of reading, the drift, exchange, Fiction, the Sentence, the new language (the one that spoke for me in a bar in Tangier), the language before last.

Souris: Mouse. M.S. reports the following: In mice, experiments have isolated their pleasure centre. If you attach an electrode to it, connected to a pedal, then the mouse will pedal and pedal until exhausted—until, indeed, it dies of pleasure (Cyrano de Bergerac would have turned this into fiction, for did he not devise fables based on taking a common metaphor *literally*—'dying of sorrow', for example?). And in the mouse's brain, a few microns from the pleasure centre, is apparently to be found the punishment centre. I have nothing to say about this story, yet it continues to enchant me.

Tumescences: Tumescences. The Text cannot be said to be a fetish object, insofar as it is directly the phallus, i.e. that which becomes monumentally erect. The text should be read, then, in terms of tumescences.

art press 4 (May–June 1973)

Writing

This short text was the preface to *La Civili-sation de l'écriture* (Writing-Based Civiliza-tion) by Roger Druet and Herman Grégoire (Paris: Fayard / Dessain et Tolra, 1976). It was reprinted in *Les Nouvelles littéraires* of 3 February 1977 as part of a section entitled 'Faire un livre'.

Given Barthes's interest in the materi-ality of writing, we should perhaps note here that Druet is one of France's most emi-nent calligraphers, typographers and graphic artists, whose work has often been exhibited in France's museums. When this book was written, he was teaching at the École supérieure des arts appliqués.

Oeuvres complètes, Volume 4, pp. 983–4

I have often wondered why I liked to write (manually, I mean), to such a degree that the often thankless effort of intellectual work has on many occasions been redeemed in my eyes by the pleasure of having before me (like the handyman's bench) a fine sheet of paper and a good pen. At the same time as I am thinking about what I am to write (this is what is happening at this very moment), I feel my hand acting, turning, connecting, going down, lifting up and very often, as corrections are made, striking something out or breaking up a line, expanding the space into the margin and in this way, with slender, apparently functional strokes (letters), constructing a space that is quite simply the space of art. I am an artist not through crafting an object but more fundamentally because, in writing, my body thrills to tracing something out, to rhythmically incising a blank surface (blankness offering infinite possibility).

That pleasure must be an ancient one—series of regularly spaced incisions have been found on the walls of certain prehistoric caves. Was that already writing? Not at all. Those marks no doubt had no meaning, but their very rhythm denoted a conscious activity that was probably magical or, more broadly, symbolic: it was the—controlled, organized or sublimated (what does it matter?)—trace of a drive. The human desire to incise (with an engraver's point, reed pen, stylus or fountain pen) or to caress (with a brush or felt-tip) has no doubt gone through a great succession of forms that have come to mask the strictly corporeal origins of writing. But it only takes a painter to incorporate graphic forms into his work from time to time (such as [André] Masson or [Cy] Twombly today) to bring us up against the obvious truth that writing is not just a technical activity but also a bodily practice of bliss [*jouissance*].

If I have given pride of place to this motif, I have done so precisely because it is ordinarily censored. This doesn't mean that the invention and development of writing weren't determined by the most pressing historical forces—by the movement of social and economic history. We know that in the Mediterranean area (by contrast with the Asiatic region), writing arose from commercial pressures—the development of agriculture and the need to build up reserves of grain forced human beings to invent a way of memorizing the objects required by any community that attempts to control the time of preservation and the space of distribution. This was how writing was born, at least in our part of the world.

The technique represented the first beginnings, then, of what we would today call economic planning. It hence became, quite naturally, a crucial instrument of power or, if you will, a *privilege* (in the social sense of the term); the writing technicians—the lawyers, scribes and priests—formed a caste (if not a class) devoted to the Ruler (and he saw to it that this was the case). Writing was for a long period an instrument of secrecy: the possession of writing marked out an area of separation, domination and controlled transmission—in short, a path of initiation. Writing has historically been linked to class division, class struggles and (in our country) the achievements of democracy.

Today, at least in our countries, everyone writes. Does this mean writing no longer has a history? Is there nothing more to be said about it? Not at all. One of the respects in which Roger Druet's book is interesting is the emphasis it places on the still very enigmatic change that comes over writing once it becomes mechanized. It is too early to say what modern man invests of his own person in this new writing, in which the hand has no part—the hand perhaps, though certainly not the eye. The body retains its connection with writing through the vision it has of it—there is a typographical aesthetic. Every book is useful, then, that teaches us to leave behind the idea of simple reading and induces us to see in the letter, as the ancient calligraphers did, the enigmatic projection of our own body.

Preface to Roger Druet and Herman Grégoire,
La Civilisation de l'écriture (Paris: Fayard /
Dessain et Tolra, 1976)

Responses

The following text, extracted from Luc Decaunes's work *Clefs pour la lecture* (Paris: Seghers, 1976) is part statement, part interview, on the subject of reading.

Oeuvres complètes, Volume 4, pp. 1016–18

Decaunes was a prolific poet and anthologist. In his youth he frequently met the Surrealist poets, including Paul Éluard, whose daughter Cécile he married. He published a number of collections and anthologies of poetry with Les Éditions Seghers, which was incorporated into the Robert Laffont publishing group in 1969.

Decaunes had been the editor of the 'Clefs' series at Seghers for ten years when he published *Clefs pour la lecture*, his first contribution to the series, a book the publisher's blurb described as 'a survey the like of which has not been seen before'. Alongside Barthes, the novelist Michel Butor and the actor and theatre director Jean Vilar are interviewed in the book, as are a number of members of the general public, in an effort to establish a picture of reading habits in France.

What does reading mean? It means being entrusted with decoding a message that has been encoded by someone else. But in reality, though we know the subject who encoded the message well, we know the decoding subject badly, and I mean 'subject' here in the very strong, psychoanalytic sense of the term. There is an enormous disparity between what we know about writing and what we know—or, rather, don't know—about reading. We have quite an extensive body of knowledge about the encoding of writing—and have had it since Antiquity—in the form, roughly speaking, of rhetoric. Rhetoric is the science that encodes the sending of messages, writing. And opposite this, on the reading side, we have nothing— no science, no art—that corresponds to rhetoric. And this has an enormous impact on our conception of literature, since we have up to this point conceived literature always as an author's art, never as a reader's. We do indeed say, in abstract terms, that the reader is the brother of the author: '*Hypocrite lecteur, mon semblable, mon frère.*' Yet this is, in reality, a kind of pious wish; we imagine that the reader is like the author and that we can apply what we say about the author to the reader. But this is mistaken. In fact, we currently have neither a rhetoric nor a psychology (in the modern sense of the term) of the reader, by which I mean a body of thought that regards the reader as truly the subject of the act of reading and hence someone who enters into dialogue with the author, not so much through reactions of an affective or psychological type, but by genuinely entering into dialogue with him at the very level of the text. This isn't just a problem of a more or less passive or active reaction, but a problem of how operations are conducted, for reading is an operation, a strategy. I will declare that, so far as I am aware, this art of reading—taking the word *art* in the very strong sense of technique—doesn't exist. And I think it will be possible only when we have completely changed our conception of the written text, of literature and of writing along lines that we can now begin to map out thanks to the advances of linguistics and, we might say, of linguistics applied precisely to literature.

I made reference at the beginning of this chapter to the 'universes' of reading. These universes aren't defined simply by subject and genres; they are something more—*and something totally different from what we find in life. The real we grasp through reading is, in fact, a figured real, a real expressed by language, and, as it were,* become *language. And that language itself is something we perceive only through the medium of writing or, in other words, of conventional signs, silent signs, which represent it visually. In these circumstances, we may already wonder whether the language we find in reading, after its passage through*

signs, is identical to oral language, the language of every-
day life or whether it has, in fact, undergone a mutation.

That is a very big question. And if there's a criterion
we can apply to the distinction between good and bad
literature, this is precisely it. Let's say that the good
written text is the one which has always incorporated
the 'subject' of reading into the elaboration of the message. In the literary texts and writings of less high quality, when he encodes his message the author doesn't
foresee and doesn't entirely master all the meanings of
that message. The meaning of an ensemble of signs is
something extremely difficult to master in its totality.
Meaning bursts out on all sides. There are parasitical
meanings, there are secondary, simultaneous, latent
meanings and, ultimately, many authors are unable to
master the totality of the meanings of what they write.
These parasitic, secondary meanings that aren't necessarily under control are what we may broadly term *connotations*: they are superimposed meanings and it's
quite clear that, when we read, we receive the connotations deliberately put into the text by the author but
we also add an infinity of connotations—that is to say,
of deep meanings—that emanate either from our culture, from our social level, from our national history,
from our social background or even, simply, from our
affective situation.

But what relations, then, does that 'figured real' which we
perceive through a coded language have with objective
reality?

Simplifying matters, we may say that for centuries—that is to say, until the discoveries of linguistics and its recent developments—we pretty much imagined the encoding—and hence the decoding—process as a rather simple operation. On one side, there was the real, whatever it was, and, on the other, the expression of the real. Language was conceived as an instrument serving to express or figure—in short, to transmit—the real, in a more or less simulative, though transformed way. Particularly since the work of Saussure, however, a third term has been introduced into this pattern which had, until that point, been a two-term schema with the real on one side and expression or language on the other. A very important third term has been introduced, though not all its consequences are evident yet, and this term is the *signified*. Language is made with signifieds and signifiers but it isn't made directly with the real. There is a certain mental operation which already transforms the real into a signified before transforming it into a sign. This means, to a certain extent, that one can no longer innocently confuse the substance (or content) of a message with the real, as was previously the case. It is something else. There is already a transformation, a transition from the real to the substance, to contents, to concepts. Language is a system that has its own economy, a dual economy in that it is articulated both to signifieds (or contents) and to signifiers (or forms); and the system holds together perfectly well, without resting—as a system—on the real. We can see here a possible opportunity to recast entirely a notion that has dominated not only literature but even psychology and communications for centuries—namely, the notion of 'realism'. Of its nature, language is never realist because it always interposes, between the form and the real, that kind of operation or internal form that is the signified. Contrary to the way we normally talk about these things, reading—that is to say, language that is written and received—doesn't *show* us some scene. It's a misuse of language to say that a description shows something. In reality, it shows nothing at all, and what it gives us of the real it gives us along a totally independent and autonomous pathway which is one of pure intelligibility. This doesn't exclude, as we have said, affective and emotive connotations, but it isn't a figurative pathway. Language refers to the real, but it doesn't express it.

From Luc Decaunes, *Clefs pour la lecture*
(Paris: Seghers, 1976)

A Kind of
Manual Labour

This was another occasional piece for *Les Nouvelles littéraires*, the long-running French literary magazine. A response to its survey on 'Writing with a Tape Recorder', it was published on 3 March 1977.

Oeuvres complètes, Volume 5, pp. 392–3

On 7 January 1977, Barthes had delivered his inaugural lecture at the Collège de France. In early April, his book *Fragments d'un discours amoureux* (Paris: Seuil, Collection 'Tel Quel'; available in English as *A Lover's Discourse: Fragments*) would appear and he would be interviewed by Claude Bonnefoy for *Les Nouvelles littéraires* of 21 April 1977.

I have a longstanding inclination to regard writing and speech as opposites in theoretical terms, since they don't seem to me to issue from the same body. It has been my view that speech came out of the body as something immediately expressive, intimidatory or seductive—in short, as theatre. Writing, by contrast, has always seemed to me to be free from any imaginary element (the concern for the other's image or one's own), because it is stripped down and at the same time hemmed in by a whole slew of codes that function as so many mediations: style, concision, ambiguity and the patience of the hand that cannot move as quickly as thought. On these grounds I would never have agreed to speak a text before writing it: interviews (of the tape-recorded variety) are something I've always granted, as we say in French, *à mon corps defendant*— that is to say, with literally corporeal reluctance.

I am less sure about this opposition today. I have in mind that writers of the past, such as Flaubert or Gide, attributed creative value to declaiming their sentences. And I know writers today who write, if I can put it that way, using a tape recorder. This makes me inclined to be liberal and believe that everyone should write with the body he has in the way he feels moved to.

However, like any liberal, having expressed the respect owed to difference, I come back to my own weakness—I like to write and not to speak; and when I write I do so with my hand, not a typewriter. Many things determine this choice. First, there is a refusal—my body refuses to speak out loud to . . . nobody. If I am not sure there's another body listening to me, my voice is paralysed and simply won't come out at all. If, in a conversation, I find that someone isn't listening to me, I stop; and it is quite beyond me to leave a message on an answering machine (I believe I am not alone in this). To speak alone in front of a tape recorder, when every voice is made for an encounter with another person, seems to me an unbearable frustration—in such circumstances, my voice is literally *cut short* (castrated). There is nothing to be done about it, I cannot be the addressee of my own voice—which is what use of the tape recorder would mean—whereas my writing is immediately produced for everyone. And then the very slowness of writing protects me—I have the time to pull back from the stupid word that never fails, in ordinary circumstances, to produce a sense of 'spontaneity'; there is a great distance between my head and my hand, and I take advantage of that distance to say something different from what initially came to mind. Lastly—and this is perhaps the real reason for my preference—from writing words on paper I derive a real physical delight [*jouissance plastique*]. If my voice gave me pleasure, that would merely be from narcissism. But, for me, writing by hand is akin to what painting is for the painter. Writing comes from my muscles and I find delight in a kind of manual labour. I combine two 'arts' here: the art of composition and the art of handwriting.

To take all this on board, one probably has to subscribe to the idea of a plurality of languages. Personally, I consider it a good thing that there are several quite separate French languages, in particular one conveyed in speech and another in writing. I believe that the existence of an artificial language which exists only through writing is a luxury that should be defended—the existence of a language made immediately to be *seen*.

Les Nouvelles littéraires (3 March 1977)

Foreword to
'Jakobson'

This brief text from 1978 provided an introduction to the special issue of the *Cahiers Cistre* on linguist Roman Jakobson. This was the fifth issue of that revue, which was originally announced as a quarterly publication but seems, in practice, to have appeared less regularly. Other numbers were devoted to Polish writer Witold Gombrowicz, psychoanalyst Jacques Lacan and Nobel Prize–winning biologist Jacques Monod. The short-lived *Cahiers Cistre* (*cistre* means cittern or cithren, a Renaissance stringed instrument generally thought to have derived from the medieval citole) were published by L'Age d'Homme, a publishing house founded in Lausanne in 1966 by the Yugoslav exile Vladimir Dimitrijevič.

Barthes begins this piece along the same lines as the earlier tribute he published in *Le Monde* in 1971 (see pp. 147–51). There he spoke of Jakobson offering literature *un très beau cadeau* (a very fine gift); here he writes of *un cadeau merveilleux*.

Oeuvres complètes, Volume 5, pp. 491–2

Roman Jakobson presented us with a marvellous gift—he gave linguistics to artists. He it was who created the living, tangible connection between one of the most demanding human sciences and the world of creation. Both by his theoretical thinking and his personal commitments he represents the meeting of scientific and creative thought.

Jakobson is the first to make an astonishing assertion for a linguist—language, he says, doesn't exist without literature and literature is its utopia. This shows how necessary it is to get beyond the facile opposition between spontaneity and coding. Poetry, for example, is an activity of super-coding or secondary coding. But it is through this coding that drives, fantasies and the world of dreams insinuate themselves. Poetry goes, in fact, to the limits of language. What is at the limit only manifests the essence the more clearly. To venture a rather risky comparison, it would seem that the idea of God has been developed in much greater depth by mystics—that is to say, by people who placed themselves on the fringe of the phenomenon of religion—than by orthodox theologians. It is the same with poetry. The poet, says Jakobson, expresses what the linguistic excludes from language [*la langue*]. In terms of the Saussurian dichotomy, poetry is part of *parole*, not *langue*. At the same time, that *parole* is coded and hence becomes *langue* once again. In his way, Saussure had sensed that there was here, in his system, what we might colloquially term a 'hitch', since there are, in fact, instances of *parole* that are coded and it isn't clear how to classify them. We don't know whether they are elements of *parole* or of *langue*. Poetic speech acts are *paroles*, but these *paroles* are coded as elements of *langue*. It is this kind of enigmatic dialectic Jakobson is getting at. Reading him, we notice the extent to which he has prevented linguistics from becoming a rigidly mechanical discipline.

It is through the interstices of form and through certain phenomena of textuality akin to schizophrenic structures that creativity passes. Now, Jakobson is one of the first to have delved perceptively into the relations between schizophrenia and poetry, most notably in respect of [Friedrich] Hölderlin. In so doing, he paved the way for the development of this field.

Criticism on the one side and the writer on the other—it seems to me we are heading towards a blurring of these functions that were hitherto kept separate. In the future there will simply be a single producer of texts, abolishing genres. The distinction will be between the 'scientists', who will be in the realm of '*écrivance*'—that is to say, they will have a purely instrumental relation to their language—and the others who, whatever they do, be it fiction, theory or philosophy, will have a relation of bliss [*jouissance*] to their language. We already know which linguistic operators will make the difference. They have to do with metaphor. There are people who write with metaphors and others who write without. This is where the dividing line will run.

But there remains the open question: Why do some people practice the perversion that is writing [*écriture*]? How do they find a profitable source of bliss in the practice of writing? This is a problem for which we have no answer as yet. There is a bliss in writing. What will it consist in? We don't know. Psychoanalysis has never really concerned itself with writing; that is one of its weak points. Bliss fans out into different practices, including writing. But it isn't substitutive: it coexists—and is consistent—with the other forms of bliss, in keeping with the very definition of poetry given by Roman Jakobson.

Cahiers Cistre 5 (L'Age d'Homme, 1978).

Relations between Fiction and Criticism according to Roger Laporte

This brief article on the French author Roger Laporte was published in *Digraphe* of April 1979. It appears to have originated in a contribution Barthes made to a radio programme entitled 'Entretiens avec R. Laporte', though this was not broadcast until some time later, on 29 May 1975, by the France Culture radio station. As already mentioned, the editor of *Digraphe* was Jean Ristat, the journal's founder (the name of the journal is said to have been suggested by Derrida).

At about this time, Barthes was working on *La Chambre Claire* (*Camera Lucida*), which he is generally thought to have written between 15 April and 3 June 1979. It was published in the following January.

Oeuvres complètes, Volume 5, pp. 758–9

et's say I'm taking advantage of an opportunity here, since Roger Laporte has just published, in Flammarion's *Textes* series, a collection of articles that are traditionally described as critical, since each one relates to a different author who is different from Roger Laporte himself. This collection is called *Quinze variations sur un thème biographique*—fifteen variations on a biographical theme. I should like to say in a word—or, rather, in two words, since I have two arguments to present—why this extremely clear work is important. And, let me add in passing, that there's a clarity that's very much Roger Laporte's own: I would say that Laporte's writing is a clear diction.

Now, ordinarily, the view is that the critic, the literary critic, is someone who likes to see himself in the author he is discussing—to project himself into that author, as they say. He's thought to have peculiar affinities with him or her and, being unable to produce good original work himself, at least to find his own voice reflected in work written by someone else. And, as received opinion has it (and literature has its own), all commentary is ultimately parasitic. It's not, I think, some bold flourish of independence or originality that causes Laporte to contest this view of the critic. It's quite simply because it is wrong. The relationship of critic to author is in no sense projective, in no way imaginary. The author isn't an other person with whom I, the critic, can be said to be enamoured in some way or to have fallen in love; the author isn't an image. What is he, then, for the critic? What are René Char, Artaud, [Franz] Kafka, [Maurice] Blanchot and [Marcel] Proust for Roger Laporte? Quite simply, a desire—the desire to write. I quote Laporte himself: 'Pure reading, reading that doesn't prompt other writing is something that is incomprehensible to me and probably always has been. I am interested only—though in that case passionately—in the works that have made me want to write.' Such, then, is the circuit of writing: the other's writing attracts me, both as model and as lack; I am, contradictorily, seduced and dissatisfied. I want literally to make good that writing—that is to say, to complement it and supplant it—and it's in this movement of love and reality that my desire to write is formed. Laporte in fact states clearly—and here I quote him again—that 'Reading Proust, Blanchot, Kafka and Artaud didn't make me want to write about those authors, but made me want to write.' So this says it all—the critic seems to practice a transitive form of writing. He 'handles' an author the way we might handle material transitively, but what he produces is actually an intransitive writing— this is writing as a verb without an object; writing the desire to write. In other words, the author he is writing about is his indirect object; that author offers the necessary detour that enables him to make free with his writing. And that doesn't, of course, prevent him from being able to speak about an author who isn't, for him, a pretext but, much more violently—as Laporte himself says—a mediator of desire. And if it turns out that for such a subject (in this case, Roger Laporte himself), life—his life—is entirely, fundamentally and I would say structurally bound up in the desire to write, then we can understand that what happens to this desire—the adventures of this desire—comes gradually to form the true *biography* of this subject; and, in consequence, his so-called critical articles are actually variations on a biographical—and, I would say, almost erotographic— theme.

Another prejudice relating to literary critics has them excluded, by their very nature, from the pantheon of true writers. Only Sainte-Beuve is celebrated in the literary textbooks and, ultimately, the future scriptor is always called upon to choose between being a novelist, in which case he will be fully a writer, or a critic, in which case he will be a poor relation of the glorious family, its mere historiographer. Roger Laporte argues, to the contrary, mildly but insistently, that, within this writing subject that he is—and that he turns himself into through desire—fiction and criticism, the literary work and the article are duplicates of the same activity; that they exist in a state of superimposition. Reading the work of fiction, one can divine the critical article, reconstitute it, recognize it. Conversely (this, at least, is the attestation I would like to add to Laporte's correct thesis), in the weft of the purely critical work, we are called on to discern—and, if possible, delight in—the thread of a fiction. It is at the very moment that, historically, so to speak, the novel seems to be disappearing from our active culture, when the classical distinction between literary genres seems at last to be fading, to be replaced by something new which for simplicity's sake we call the text; it is at just this moment that Roger Laporte is telling us: 'Within what each of us writes, try to make out the fiction of writing that is its origin and its attraction.' And because Roger Laporte's articles have exactly the same tone, the same diction, the same elegance and, if I may put it this way, the same scrupulousness as his free texts—in a word, literally the same writing [*écriture*]—we understand that, in his remarkable works, everything is written to surpass itself and to unname itself, so that all that remains is that enigmatic thing, both tender and abstract, anonymous and inimitable, distinct and fluent, which is, paradoxically, the whole substance of Roger Laporte's writing and which we may call a voice.

Digraphe (April 1979), special issue on Roger Laporte